SELF WORK

OVERCOME ANY STRUGGLE, DEVELOP SELF-DISCIPLINE & FULFULL YOUR MAXIMUM POTENTIAL

Terri Andres

HARVESTER PUBLISHING
ATLANTA, GA

Copyright © 2020 by Terri Andres.

All rights reserved. No part of this publication may be reproduced, distributed or transmitted in any form or by any means, including photocopying, recording, or other electronic or mechanical methods, without the prior written permission of the publisher, except in the case of brief quotations embodied in critical reviews and certain other noncommercial uses permitted by copyright law. For permission requests, write to the publisher, addressed "Attention: Permissions Coordinator," at the address below.

Terri Andres/Harvester Publishing
4780 Ashford Dunwoody Rd
Atlanta, Georgia
harvester-publishing.com

Book cover design by Tanya Prokop.

Ordering Information:
Bulk sales. Special discounts are available on bulk purchases by organizations, small groups and others. For more info, email support@harvester-publishing.com.

Self Work/ Terri Andres. —1st ed.
ISBN 978-1-7351862-0-7

Contents

About This Book and Coaching 7

Introduction 13

    BIG COACHING MOMENT LET'S GET CLEAR 14

Section I - Overcome Any Struggle

Real Life = Real Struggles 19

What Does Winning Look Like for You? 23

Ground Zero: Truth 29

Bridging the Gap: Where You Are and Where You Want to Be 33

ACT Now: Defusing Wrong Thoughts 37

Will: Conviction, Desire, Decision, Power & Control ... 43

Feelings: Unfriendly Foes 51

Soul Work Recap + Conclusion 57

    BIG COACHING MOMENT LET'S GET CLEAR 58

Section II - Develop Self-Discipline

Discipline is Better 62

    BIG COACHING MOMENT LET'S GET CLEAR 64

The Mind-Body Connection 67

Discipline of The Mind 73

The Discipline of Self-Sacrifice 83
Body Behavior 99
Soul Self-Discipline 117
Self-Governance 125
Food for Thought 127
Making Up When You Mess You 135
Body Work Recap + Conclusion 139
   BIG COACHING MOMENT LET'S GET CLEAR..... 142

Section III - Fulfill Your Maximum Potential

Your Highest and Best Self 147
   BIG COACHING MOMENT LET'S GET CLEAR..... 148

Identifying Your Thing 151
How to Start Thriving 155
Handling Resistance 167
Having More Energy 179
Maximum Potential Recap + Conclusion 187
   BIG COACHING MOMENT LET'S GET CLEAR..... 190

*Dedicated to
all who are committed to self work*

Man's greatest hindrance is self.

—UNKNOWN

Outside of a higher power one subscribes to, man's greatest asset is self.

—TERRI ANDRES

About This Book and Coaching

This book is a personal coaching guide that is designed to coach you in improving some area or areas of yourself.

What exactly is meant by coaching? Life coaching, as defined by the International Coach Federation (the gold standard in coaching across the globe) is *partnering with clients in a thought-provoking and creative process that inspires them to maximize their personal and professional potential.*

Coaches keep their clients motivated and committed and they ask powerful questions to help them achieve their goals.

Coaching differs significantly from counseling in that coaches believe in their client and believe they have the answers to their own problems or obstacles within them. Too, unlike counselors, the coach is not a subject expert. Rather, the coach's role and focus is on helping clients unlock their own potential.

Think of a life coach as being like a sport team coach. The player is the one with all the gifts, talent and skill, as well as the one who does the hard work. The coach serves to draw out the greatness the player possesses by strategically leading, encouraging, motivating and supporting him or her play by play for the win.

Coaching is an effective and powerful way to achieve any personal, professional, relationship, financial, health, educational, athletic or any kind of goal, as well as catapult you to your next level.

My encouragement and challenge for you is to believe in the dynamic power of coaching to transform your being and life.

Now let's talk a little about the mechanics of coaching and, in particular, personal coaching to increase your understanding and learn how to best coach yourself using the coaching I've integrated throughout the book.

Remember, coaching is a highly effective way to achieve goals. Any goal. By in large, people who are interested in coaching and invest in coaching are people who, not only want to achieve a goal they have set for themselves but are serious (keyword) about achieving their goal or goals.

Coaching causes you to get crystal clear about your goal. Coaching causes you to come up with a viable action plan for your goal by an identified time. Coaching keeps you accountable, motivated and focused on the journey to achieving your goal. Coaching also strengthens your resiliency to overcome and recover from inevitable obstacles and/or setbacks along the way.

There are dozens of coaching methods in existence today from industry regulating federations, top professional organizations and from coaches themselves who have defined these methods.

Myself included.

As a professionally certified personal and executive coach, I have used my knowledge, skill and experience coaching clients to create the coaching model that will be used here. The name of it is GROW[2] and it is designed specifically for *self-coaching*. Not life coaching. Not business coaching. Not career coaching. Not relationship coaching. Not financial coaching or any other type of coaching.

Self-coaching centers around self and is a tool for self work, which I have broken down into two major parts: soul work and body work. I will, of course, unpack both as we go along but, for now, here is a brief summary of each.

Soul work includes:
- Your mind (heart, belief, intellect, intelligence, perceptions, reasoning, imagination, visualization)
- Your will (convictions, actions, habits)
- Your feelings (affections, emotions, fear, offense, unforgiveness, hatred, pride, happiness, joy, sadness, surprise, disgust, frustration, anxiety, anger)

Body work includes:
- Your physical condition (health, fitness, etc.)
- Your behavior (self-control, self-discipline, etc.)
- Your intake and consumption (food/drink, intimacy, sexual activity, etc.)

If you are reading this, know you are a living, breathing soul with a body and the unseen parts of your being are superior and what control the parts of you that can be seen (i.e., your body and your behavior).

Take some time to earnestly consider the current condition of each of these aspects of your self. And the key phrase here is *the current condition*. This is a big idea I want you to grasp.

When you get ready to make a major purchase such as a house, or car, or boat, or vacation home or some other large possession, you assess the current condition of it – especially if it is something preowned. You hire out or do your own homework to determine whether the condition is excellent, good, decent, poor or outright bad.

Since you go through great lengths to judge and act based on the condition of external, material things, wouldn't it make just as much sense or more to go through the same or greater lengths when it comes to your own self? Of course!

This is what doing the work of self, or self work, looks like. Get the ball rolling by assessing your current conditions.

The GROW^2 Self-Coaching Model™

G	Gap analysis
	Where am I now?
	Where do I need and/or desire to be? Why?
R	Reflection
	What truth do I need to admit/come to terms with?
	What have I believed or accepted to be true but is not?
O	Obstacles
	Identify all current obstacles in your way of taking a step forward.
W	Will
	What decision or decisions will I make now?
	What commitment or commitments will I make now?
W	Work
	What do I need to do, in terms of my actions?
	What is the single most valuable and viable step I can take toward this?
	When will I do it by? Who will I be accountable to?

This simple but powerful self-coaching model should be used as a guide during the coaching moments incorporated through the book.

I encourage you to make a commitment now to go beyond merely reading and take the time to coach yourself.

Anticipate *Coaching Moments* and believe they will lead to the better self you desire. Immerse yourself in the work of these moments with the same level of earnestness you would working on a project that was going to make you a millionaire. Because, truth be told, your self is worth much more.

Introduction

You have a vision for your self and your life. And you are frustrated because that vision does not exactly line up with your current self, situation and circumstances. And it hasn't for years. And you are exhausted. Sick and tired of being sick and tired.

The problem isn't that you're not willing to change. You are. You want to change. In fact, you're desperate for change. You even know what you need to do in order to change.

So you put forth your best effort to change but ultimately fail and find yourself repeating this pattern over and over again.

Why?

Because of some inner struggle. Or because of lack of self-discipline. Or because of lack of confidence, or insecurity, in yourself which creates frustration and hinders you from fulfilling your maximum potential. Or maybe all the above.

My aim for this project was to share the best of what I have learned to be true about self in order to improve in the greatest area(s) in which your own self needs improvement.

This book is for the person who wants to become their highest and best self. The person who wants to feel and look better in their physical and mental health and well-being. The person who wants better relationships. The person who wants to manage their time and money better. The person who wants to show up better in their business and career.

If any of these are you, commit now to doing all the required work (i.e., coaching exercises) and let's get started.

BIG COACHING MOMENT
LET'S GET CLEAR

1. What do you want more of for your self?
2. What is most important to you when it comes to self work?
3. Who do you see your self as?
4. How close or far away are you?
5. Why or why not?

Before we begin, ponder and answer these powerful, clarifying coaching questions. Because, in order for your self work to be effective and produce results, it is vitally important to get crystal clear on two things: where you are now and where you want to be by the end of the book.

Too, know this and get geared up for it: that getting clear is going to require courage and honesty.

Courage and honesty to face the truth (keyword) about your current self – the good, the bad and the ugly.

Courage and honesty to confront and course correct lies and limiting beliefs.

Courage and honesty to confront and course correct bad habits and misbehaviors.

Courage to make better choices when the better path is not fun, easy, entertaining or comfortable but rather requires operating outside your comfort zone and exercising self-control by sacrificing self in some shape, form or fashion.

SECTION I:

OVERCOME ANY STRUGGLE

CHAPTER 1

Real Life = Real Struggles

Man. Woman. Boy or girl. No matter your gender, your age or your stage in life. No matter your geography or your socioeconomic status. No matter how educated or how uneducated you are. No matter how mature or how immature you are. No matter how rich or how poor you are. You have struggles.

Struggle for your very self. Your spirit, soul and body. Your love. Your joy. Your peace. Your happiness.

Struggle for the life you are living. Your purpose. Your service. Your gifts and calling. Your fruitfulness and productivity. Your work.

Struggle for your relationships. Relationships with your loved ones. Your spouse or significant other. Your children. Your parents. Your friends. Your associations. Your colleagues and/or coworkers.

Struggle for your finances. Struggle with your past failures. Struggles with your fears. Struggle with your faith or some other struggle related to your self not listed here.

Living in this present world as we know it where there is the existence of good and evil guarantee struggles for all of us. Too, because there are no perfect people. There are no perfect "selfs."

Quite the contrary, our "selfs" are imperfect and prone to messing up more often than not.

Self is man's biggest hinderance. The sole source for most of the struggles we grapple with. What is going on on the inside of us. Some hurt, habit or hang-up. Some psychological and/or soul deficit one just can't fully break free from no matter how hard he or she tries. Truth be told, the harder we try, the deeper we sink into it. These factors -- along with many other outside the scope of this book -- are what makes self work so necessary.

The contents of these pages are going to help you break free. First, knowing that freedom is a process. A process that, as you will see, requires work from every aspect of your being — spirit, soul and body.

We are going to dive deep but what I want to encourage you with here and now is this: to know that you have a choice. No matter your past or present. No matter your fault or someone else's. No matter the adversity. No matter the mistake. No matter the situation or circumstance, you have a choice to how you – your *self* – will show up and respond to people, situations and circumstances.

One thing I have learned about life is it always presents us with the opportunity to choose right. To choose the path least traveled. The narrow gate that few choose. I believe you are one of the few.

I am here to tell you that you do not have to feel bad, hurt, suffer from depression, anger, insecurity, inferiority, fear, worry, anxiety or any other stressor. I am not saying you will not stress — living in this world unfortunately involves stress. But just because you feel stressed and experience stress does not mean you have to be stressed and live in a stressful state 24/7. You don't.

Know that you have choices and they are entirely yours to make.

BITE-SIZED COACHING MOMENT

1. Are you ready, willing and wholly committed to doing the work?
2. Why or why not?
3. What makes this time different from any other time you have tried to self-improve?

_____

_____

_____

_____

_____

_____

_____

CHAPTER 2

What Does Winning Look Like for You?

If I know right, I know you know exactly what winning would look like for your *self*. You've imagined it over and over and over again because you have hope that one day you will be the greater self you see yourself as and, as such, do all the great things you see yourself doing.

Research backs this up. According to Dr. Jennice Vilhaur, Director of Emory University's Adult Outpatient Psychotherapy Program in the Department of Psychiatry and Behavioral Science in the School of Medicine, your brain is constantly using visualization in the process of simulating future experiences.

This process happens so naturally that many people generally are not even aware of it. It becomes second nature akin to breathing. This becomes interesting because, if a person is not aware of it then they are not actively directing the process. The good news is, anyone can learn to use (i.e., actively direct) visualization to create future simulations of themselves and circumstances.

There are two types of simulations, outcome and process. An outcome simulation is a sensory-based representation of the final outcome you expect, and a process situation involves simulating the steps that get you to the final outcome.

Studies show that to get the most benefit from simulations, it is best to use both types together. Further, creating your simulation using the participant perspective instead of the observer perspective has been shown to be more effective. You want to see yourself as a part of the simulated experience.

Why is this important? Because using simulation can improve your motivation and increase your belief in your ability to win. To achieve any goal. To overcome any struggle with self.

The Power of Visualization

Psychologists have been using visual imagery for years to help people enhance performance at skill-based activities, create desired emotional states, and achieve life goals.

People who want to learn to shoot basketball hoops can show considerable improvement just by visualizing shooting baskets in their heads. Simply visualizing playing the piano can actually improve someone's ability to play a piece. In other words, being able to do something in your head, greatly increase your changes of being able to do it in real life.

Within this context, recalling the well-known bible teaching *as a man thinks in his heart so is he*, we can accurately conclude the power of visualization not only applies to performance but it also applies to states of being.

Which is to say, we can use our thoughts to visualize the self we desire to be and in doing so actually be working – as the ancient wisdom and scientific research alike shows -- toward our future self by this very action. Wow. What a profound picture of self work.

Visualization in Action

There are three different types of visualization techniques that can be employed to increase the quality of your mental simulations.

1. **Picture and Describe.** This is all about painting the picture. The more details you have for your visualization the more real it will seem and the more it will increase actions as your brain starts to develop neural connections that result from the repeated visual images. In a nutshell, this motivates and moves you toward your goal.

2. **Emotional Intensity.** Since emotions are preceded by thoughts, when you feel something deeply, you have achieved a level of belief associated with it. You generally don't feel very upset by something that you know is absolutely unreal or true. This is why we can watch upsetting fictional events on TV and in film but not truly be traumatized. However, the more real or true you believe something to be, the more emotional impact it has on you. To really enhance a simulation, you want to create as much detail around it as you can so that you begin to feel the experience of it as if it were real. Once you have begun to feel it, you have crossed the threshold that leads to action.

3. **Exposure.** This allows you to create a more detailed and realistic visual simulation in your mind. For example, if you really dream of doing something you've never tried before, like sky diving, you may have a difficult time simulating a detailed experience because you don't have much to draw on. You will need to increase your exposure to it by looking at educational videos, reading books or talking to sky diving instructors and people who actually sky dive. Anything that increases your knowledge in order to create your own detailed (keyword) visualization.

These techniques have been proven to make your visualizations seem more real which ultimately work to enhance motivational drive and performance.

Simple Visualization Exercise

This exercise[1] is meant to you inspire you into discovering what you need to become the self you see yourself as and to prompt creative ideas. Get into it and go with me here.

> *Sit comfortably on your chair, back erect, feet planted on the floor. Take a deep breath through your nose and exhale slowly through your mouth holding the inhale for a couple seconds before exhaling gently through your mouth.*
>
> *Imagine you are alone at the top of an extremely high mountain looking at the endless beauty and vastness before you. It is a picture-perfect clear day without a cloud in the sky. You can see and hear the sounds of nature. The sun is shining and warm on your skin. The wind is blowing gently. You feel content and ultimate satisfaction. You feel exhilarated, excited and invincible while your frame remains completely relaxed. You are standing still soaking it all in for what feels like hours.*
>
> *As you look toward the horizon you see light. The light becomes brighter and is coming toward you. By now you sense from the inside, that this light is your future self. As it gets a few yards from you, you start noticing the form within the light. It is a beautiful form of grace, beauty, confidence and friendliness – as if this person has attained all the attributes he or she wanted and is totally successful.*
>
> *There is a feeling of awesomeness as you take in all of it, and slowly you realize, it is my future self. You walk closer, and welcome and respectfully embrace your future self. You feel the energy of kindness and generosity.*
>
> *It was a simple encounter and it leaves you feeling grateful, confident and contented. You find yourself sitting on the side of the mountain, as if you had a restful time and you are very awake refreshed and know what you want to do.*

Closing power-thought: the future is not a place we are going to. It is what we are creating right now.

---

[1] This visualization exercise was used with permission from Clea Holdridge of Clear Coaching Now and was slightly modified to fit closer into our context of Self Work.

BITE-SIZED COACHING MOMENT

1. Did this visualization exercise work for you?
2. Were you able to envision your near-future self vividly?
    a. If not, why? What is the blocker?
    b. If yes, what did you learn?
3. What idea(s) did you have as it relates to your near-future self?
4. What action(s) do you need to take?
    a. What do you need to start or stop?
    b. How important is this on a scale from 1-10?

_____

_____

_____

_____

_____

_____

_____

CHAPTER 3

Ground Zero: Truth

Self work starts here. Telling yourself the truth is the bedrock for any and all self-growth and transformation for the better. Why? Because our behavior is based on our beliefs, simply defined as what we believe is true. And it is our beliefs that determine our thoughts, which determine our actions, which determine our outcomes within and outside of ourselves. Good or bad.

With this in mind, we can see how vitally important truth is – understanding that the truth I am speaking of here should not be confused with what someone believes is true. Because we all know how dangerously easy it is to believe something is true when, in fact, it is not. We witness this and its undesirable (often tragic) consequences all through life and have likely experienced some degree of this ourselves.

So back to you. In order to overcome what you are struggling with, the first thing you must do is make the connection back to truth. Mostly every struggle with self stems from not knowing, ignoring or rejecting truth and thus causing your actions (struggle) to be based on some type of deception.

Why is acting based on truth and not deception such a big deal? The short answer is because of good and evil.

Truth is good and deception is evil. As such, actions based on truth are good (healthy, constructive and fruitful) whereas actions based on deception are evil (harmful, destructive and fruitless). Meditate on this until you really get it.

How We Get Deceived

Life lies to us. This corrupt world. The cultures we are conditioned in. The people in our family and other influencers that have been lied to and pass down their wrong beliefs and perceptions to us. Bad guys out for no good and so on.

Too, because we want what we want when we want it, we convince ourselves that this or that is right and ok – "as long as we're not hurting anyone" – and end up accepting our personal beliefs as truth without even realizing that we've made them to be true when in fact they are not. We manufacture "truth."

The enormous danger in this, again, goes back to this big idea of good and evil. If you are not acting based on truth (good) you are acting based on deception (evil) and your outcomes are one or the other.

Let's pretend your struggle is smoking cigarettes or marijuana. At some point you convinced yourself that smoking was ok– regardless of the specific story you told yourself. So, you smoked and smoked and smoked until the point came where you are no longer in control of what you are consuming. Rather, what you are consuming is now consuming you and you are addicted. To your dismay.

The story you told yourself about it being ok was the personal belief you accepted as truth but really wasn't and so you acted – smoked without reservation or hesitation – based on deception which brought forth evil (a bad habit and addiction that is harmful to your mental and physical health).

If the story you told yourself had been the truth – that smoking is harmful and addictive – your actions would have been based on truth and brought forth good (not smoking and subsequent addiction to it).

Recently, I was talking to a loved one about something I am honestly hard-pressed to remember right now but we had differing views on the subject. In short, I was speaking truth and he did not want to hear or receive it. But I distinctly remember thinking and then saying, *I am going to stand up for God and speak truth regardless of your rejection of it!* Thankfully, our discussion did not turn into an argument because he came around relatively quickly. Why? Because I stood strong and didn't shrink to my conviction to always speak the truth no matter what or who.

I share this because it is one example of millions that show the way of truth is not the often road traveled. It is the narrow road that few choose to follow. Because, as the saying goes, the truth hurts. It disagrees and opposes our self-centeredness and selfish wants.

But when we pause to reflect. When we get real and honest. When we tap into our higher, nobler selves. We will admit that the way we have been doing things is not working great for us. We will admit that we like to think that we know what is best for us but the truth is we don't always know what is best for us – especially when we are deceived.

The truth is, our untruthful ways of doing things is what is keeping us struggling and stuck where we are.

MEDIUM-SIZED COACHING MOMENT

1. Think of a time when you believed something was true and later found out it was not. What were the consequences?
2. Is your struggle (ill-actions) based on truth or based on some deception? Explain.
3. What do you need to acknowledge as the truth – the real root cause of your struggle. State what is true.

_____

_____

_____

_____

_____

_____

_____

_____

_____

CHAPTER 4

Bridging the Gap: Where You Are and Where You Want to Be

Thoughts are the things that bridge the gap between where you are and where you desire to be. The way you think determines your behavior. Your actions, which become habits, which determine your outcomes which, when strung together, determine the quality of your being and life.

Good habits are good habits and are great. Bad habits and bad and harmful to your health and because of this they usually become addictions which are really mental strongholds.

Now I really want you to catch that. Bad habits are in reality mental strongholds. The way you think about something that causes you to behave in a certain way.

Think of it this way. Think about your struggle. Let's say you struggle with looking at soft porn (pictures of naked women) or triple XXX porn (watching people having sex). The reason I don't have this struggle is because I think soft and XXX porn is awful on every level. It is awful for women and men to pose naked and have their picture taken. It is awful for men and women to have sex openly and have it pre-recorded or streamed live. It is awful for men, women or children to look at any of these things. You, on the other hand, at some point did not think any of these behaviors were awful on any level. Therefore, you readily and willing engaged in it. Until now, what you have been consuming has consumed you – to the point that you are now addicted to it.

Your thinking about pornography created a mental stronghold in your mind – which is defined as a spiritual fortress made of wrong thoughts. "Spiritual" because this mental fortress is unseen.

Now that you think differently about it, you must break the mental stronghold that developed in your mind by reprogramming your mind.

Just like the mental stronghold did not happen overnight, reprogramming will not happen overnight. It is a process. It is a process because of the nature of strongholds. Strongholds are fortified places. They are not easily destroyed. Even a physical fortress takes a lot of effort to deconstruct. Imagine the work – self work – it takes for a mental one.

Course Correcting

Remember there are two parts to self work: soul work and body work. The mind is a part of soul work.

So how do you change the way you think? What's the 1-2-3 step to start thinking right thoughts instead of wrong ones?

We are going to dive into the practical's and some strategies next, but something important to realize upfront is the fact that it won't be easy or overnight. In fact, it will be difficult and it will take *work*. First, it will take decision and conviction to stick to your decision. Then, mental discipline to think right when wrong thoughts invade. It is also going to take consistency and perseverance. Are you up for this?

Ask and answer the following questions. This is your commitment to doing the self work needed – no matter the cost – to smash mental strongholds and start thinking right.

BITE-SIZED COACHING MOMENT

1. Are you ready, willing and wholly committed to doing the work to start thinking the right thoughts?
2. Why or why not?
3. What makes this time different from any other time you've tried to self-improve in this area?

_____

_____

_____

_____

_____

_____

CHAPTER 5

ACT Now: Defusing Wrong Thoughts

In Acceptance and Commitment Therapy, or ACT for short, cognitive defusion is the process of getting unstuck from our thoughts. Wrong thoughts. More on this in a moment.

What I have found from my own struggles overcoming lies, limiting beliefs, irrational fears, and other mental ills, to be the foremost truth about wrong thoughts is that mostly all of it exists only in our minds.

Profound, I know (joke).

Did you know that thoughts are a byproduct of brain function? Thoughts — any thought whether good or bad — is proof that your brain is working. Because of this, we are not able to directly control thoughts we have (we can indirectly control this to a degree by our input, or what we choose to feed on).

> *While we have no control over what thoughts come to our mind, we have all the control over what we do with them. What our response will be.*

For example, you cannot control having an ill thought of killing yourself when you are going through an extremely painful situation. Or thinking how much you hate yourself because of the color of your skin; or your natural build being thick or thin; or for having a big nose; or for being extremely tall or short; or for some other God-given physical attribute that you you've come to despise because you have, over a long period of time, accepted these negative, ill and hateful thoughts about yourself as truth.

Cognitive defusion deals with this.

In *Learning to Thrive*, Giulia Suro, PhD tells us "when we get so entangled with our thoughts and stories about things that we believe and do what they tell us more than we believe what is really true – based on reality and actual lived experience – we are in a state of mind called *cognitive fusion*. We are fused with, or stuck to, our cognitions. Our thoughts.

The problem with getting fused in this way is that our thoughts aren't always very reliable. They show up as though they are reflecting and describing reality, when in fact our minds are busy passing judgments and creating integrations that can be and often are far from accurate or true.

The key to defusion, to getting unstuck, is learning to see thoughts for what they are: by-products of having a brain."

> *Our brains produce thoughts the same way our lungs breathe air – it's what they are built for.*

I find these facts fascinating.

More on the abstract side, most of us know well that our thoughts (aka *paradigms*, aka *narratives*, aka *scripts*, aka *schemas*, aka *mindsets* and – get this – aka *life traps*!), shape our views and have the power to create our reality. A related idea important to realize is our thoughts are resistant to change and, because of this, they become self-fulfilling prophecies.

Further, there is scientific research that shows paradigms, or thoughts, can literally become parts of our bodies as well by causing changes in the brain and other systems: nervous, endocrine, digestive, and musculoskeletal.

"New technology keeps improving our ability to see the brain at work, so that science is very close to being able to trace connections between thoughts and their pathways in the brain," writes Dr. Richard O'Connor in his book *Rewire: Change your Brain to Break Bad Habits, Overcome Addictions and Conquer Self-Destructive Behavior.* "Chronic anxiety caused by unconscious fear results in damage to the hippocampus, a part of the brain that is essential to calming us down. With enough stress, nerve cells in the hippocampus begin to shrivel up and die."

Wow. I don't know about you but, for me, this little medical/scientific tidbit alone is big enough reason for me to become a very good guard over my thoughts.

ACTing Forward

So, using psychotherapy and behavioral strategies like cognitive defusion become vital.

Knowing and acting based on the knowledge that, as Dr Sura points out, "thoughts in and of themselves don't have to mean anything, and we don't have to do anything in response to them. It's when we believe them as fact and allow them to direct our behavior that we give them way more power than they should have." And down an ugly path we go.

"Over time, as you notice your thoughts coming and going, you will see that they are simply a combination of words and images that your mind produces over the course of the day." Some thoughts are very helpful, and, on the other hand, some thoughts are very unhelpful and even harmful.

With awareness of these things, we are in a better position to not confuse thoughts – especially the ill ones – with truth or reality. We can quickly and easily judge the facts. Thoughts are what they are: just thoughts that could be true or not, and most often not due to a large and diverse range of human deficiency and wonkiness.

MEDIUM-SIZED COACHING MOMENT

1. What is the most self-destructive thought you need to diffuse and get unstuck from?
2. Identify the root of this rotten fruit.
3. What new thought will begin shifting this mental paradigm from negative to positive?
4. How will you ACT from this point forward? (Regardless of what you feel or your present beliefs. Just accept where you are and commit to the new thought.)

_____

_____

_____

_____

_____

_____

CHAPTER 6

Will:
Conviction, Desire, Decision, Power & Control

Several aspects define human will. One – arguably the most significant of them all – is free will, which is your personal willingness. Your volition. What you will or will not do. The deliberate decisions and choices you make and subsequent actions you take.

Another aspect of will is the degree of power and control you have over your emotions and actions. Like having an iron will or like that of a wet noodle. A weak will.

Yet another aspect of will is when you have a strong desire and/or determination for something. Like having the will to fight for a just cause. Or having the will to win at something. Or having the will to finish a kick-butt graduate school program. Or to become a better spouse, parent, etc.

There are significantly more aspects of human will, but the ones we are going to briefly hone in on are free will, conviction, desire, decision and willpower. With the objective of strengthening your will to do whatever it takes -- despite any associated discomfort from being stretched outside your comfort zone – and to stay the course to overcome what you are struggling with.

Conviction

In general, when you think about your free will, it is easy to make the connection to your actions. Because basically, as mentioned above, your will is what you deliberately will and will not do.

But more specifically, outside of situations and circumstances where motivations to act this way or that way are easily identified, have you ever considered what else might be at play in determining your actions?

After giving this some thought, your answers may include your desires, decisions, determinations, commitments, choices and the like. Which would all be right. But there is something stronger than all of these. And that something is your convictions.

Conviction in context here is the act of convincing a person of error or compelling the admission of a truth. Or said another way, conviction is the state of being convinced of error or compelled to admit the truth.

What makes our will and subsequent actions right as opposed to wrong is our convictions.

Conviction is a huge determining factor for our actions. It operates as a forceful, compelling current within our character.

And because conviction is inherently good, strong convictions tend to produce good actions which, ultimately, produce good outcomes.

Desire

When you begin to think about desire one of the first words that should come to mind is passion. And rightfully so because the word passion really captures and encompasses the idea of desire – its definition as well as its profoundness in terms of the depths and the degrees to which it drives our human will and, in turn, our actions and, ultimately our outcomes.

With this, passion, since it is such a profound driving force and determinator, we must be careful with the passions we cultivate, or allow to grow, in us.

Realize, comprehend and act armed with the understanding that passion can be extremely self-constructive or it can be extremely self-destructive to your being and quality of life.

Decision

One of the countless life lessons my father taught me was about decisions. That making decisions is one of the things that makes you an adult. That separates the mature from the immature. Children don't make earnest decisions. Adults do.

Much can be said about the importance and power of this subject. We know many books and white papers from scholarly study and psychological and scientific research have been authored.

Within scope here, I want to share two simple thoughts. The first is to realize the distinction between your decision (mindset) and decisions (actions). The second is to realize, comprehend and act with the understanding that it is a privilege to make a decision. Be intentional and work at growing in wisdom so you can use this great privilege wisely when exercising your free will. It will serve you well. #fact

Power & Control

Possessing the power to control your self. Possessing. The. Power (keyword). To. Control (keyword). Your. Self (keyword).

Power. Control. Self.

Major keywords that capture the essence of these vital attributes that ought to be part of the description of your will and exercise of it.

You can also think of it like you think of *willpower,* which I bet rings a bell because it is the orthodox, or normal, reference to this.

To define it here, our simple definition is *the power to decide or control emotions or actions.* For example, when a person decides to quit smoking cigarettes cold turkey. The exercise of willpower can be clearly seen.

So, what's the bottom line?

We must be able to control our will when situations or circumstances are outside our favor. We must also be able to control our will in order to effectively deal with brokenness of our inner selves from childhood hurts and traumas that most of us have carried into adulthood and have not served us well because they've formed (or better said, malformed) our perceptions, actions and everything in between. The results of which are all sorts of struggles and self-sabotage.

But what if wounded souls possessed enough personal power to control negative and reckless thoughts, decisions, and actions? There would be different, better outcomes not only for his- or herself, but for the world at large.

A better world starts with a better self and a better self, among other things, start with a better human will. Make sure yours is aligned with good.

SELF WORK • 47

BITE-SIZED COACHING MOMENT

1. Think about the deliberate decisions and choices you make and subsequent actions you take consistently. Which one of these need to change? Which one of these need to change now?
2. What ought you do instead?
3. Write out your game plan for this new action.

_____

_____

_____

_____

_____

_____

_____

EXERCISE :: LOCATE YOURSELF

Now is a good time to remember and reflect on the major two areas of Self Work and to locate where you are today in each. The purpose of this exercise is to identify your current condition so you know what area you should focus most on.

I. Soul work includes:
- Your mind
    - Heart, belief, intellect, intelligence, perceptions, reasoning, imagination, visualization
- Your will
    - Convictions, desires, decisions, actions
- Your feelings
    - Affections, emotions, fear, offense, unforgiveness, hatred, pride, happiness, joy, sadness, surprise, disgust, frustration, anxiety, anger

II. Body work includes:
- Your physical condition
    - Health
    - Fitness
    - Energy
- Your behavior
    - Actions
    - Self-control (moment to moment)
    - Self-discipline (routine)
- Your intake and consumption
    - Food and drink
    - Connection with others
    - Intimacy and sexual activity

Working from left to right, place a mark on the line that represents where you are today.

	Poor Condition	Excellent Condition
My mind	_____	
My will	_____	
My feelings	_____	
My physical condition	_____	
My behavior	_____	
My intake & Consumption	_____	

CHAPTER 7

Feelings: Unfriendly Foes

Have you ever been in an awkward situation where ill-feelings were felt without a single word being spoken? Despite a word not being said, the atmosphere was full of tension or some other negative emotion Or, even a positive emotion would apply in making this point.

Could you physically see the tension, anger and/or hatred? Or, on the flip side, love and happiness? No. Because we all know we cannot see feelings. They are unseen. Yet they are very real. In fact, not only are they real, they are superior to what can be seen.

In that awkward situation, no words were necessary to make it awkward because of the unseen, superior energy of feelings that were at work.

Today, in Western culture and worldwide, to a large detriment and for far too many, feelings are taking control over entire beings.

Outlooks. Decisions. Bodies. Behaviors. Lives being lived based on feelings.

Alarmingly, value systems are being formed based on feelings and because of this bad foundation, our thoughts, actions, and ultimately, our outcomes are being shaped by our feelings.

Too many are making choices and going about their daily routines based on feelings. Acting based on how some person, or some thing, or some activity makes us feel. And, typically, the feelings bring pleasure to any one of our five senses as opposed to people, things and activities that stimulate and require cognitive energy. Simply said, doing whatever is fun, easy or entertaining versus reading, deep study, researching and writing, or earnest effort on some other type of business and professional work.

Pattern Interrupting Feelings

If the above shoes fit, for self work and getting serious about it, you need a pattern interrupt.

> *You need to move from acting from feelings to acting from faith.*

Faith being your higher hopes, dreams, aspirations, calling and purpose. Aligning your actions with what you hope for. What you dream about. What you aspire to. What you are called to. Your superior reason for being – your purpose.

I have often heard people say the opposite of faith is fear. I submit another opposite of faith is feelings. Because faith and feeling are indeed opposites.

Faith is unseen and absent of feeling. It is immaterial. Feeling, in the sense of to feel or to touch, is material. Too, feelings in the sense of emotions are, in effect, seen and felt. For instance, frustration, anxiety, anger, hatred, happiness, sadness, surprise, disgust, unforgiveness, offense, fear etc.

Feelings in the Context of Self Work

What exactly are feelings? How are they defined? These are rhetorical questions because I know you have feelings and know well what they are. Nonetheless, it can still be enlightening to read and thereby refresh our minds on what we already know. When we do, our knowledge expands. We create space for light bulb moments and, ultimately, we grow. Which is always a good thing.

Merriam-Webster's online dictionary defines feeling/feelings in the following several ways:

1. *a) One of the basic physical senses of which the skin contains the chief organs and of which the sensations of touch and temperature are characteristic. b) touch c) generalized bodily consciousness or sensation*
2. *An emotional state or reaction*
3. *Susceptibility to impression. Sensitivity*
4. *Conscious recognition. To sense*
5. *Often unreasoned opinion or belief. Sentiment*

These are good to become reacquainted with – especially because of the big (too big of) place we give our feelings. But more importantly for our objectives here, we need to contextualize feelings for self work. I really want you to have a clear picture of how feelings are ruling and ruining our beings and lives. And, because of this, why it is imperative to get control of them.

I already touched upon it at the beginning of this chapter but allow me to expound.

With respect to values, how you spend your free time is a good indication of what you value. And if the majority of your free time is spent on streaming tv series, movies or on social media sites, it reveals you value these things above (keyword) something else you proclaim to value outside of these things (say, for example, reading or writing or exercising or napping or practicing piano).

Feeling Pathways

The former of these is the Path of Least Resistance. The fun, easy and entertaining route. The route that caters to your feeling. Raw feels as referred to in Philosophy. The latter of these caters to cognitive energy and – today, like never before because of technology – is the road less traveled.

How we look at things. Our outlooks. Our perspectives are too much based on feeling and whether we will gain some sort of pleasurable material benefit.

Our decisions and choices. Our will when it comes to how we manage our relationships, how we manage our external affairs and how we manage our time – creator or consumer. Essentially, how we steward our lives. Too much our decisions and choices trace back to

Our bodies and behavior. Our will when it comes to managing our selves. Our self-control and self-discipline. Too much, we seek to feel some form of pleasure. Whether it be from some person (having casual sex), some thing (food, sugar, drugs, drinking) or some activity (streaming entertainment, social media, watching soft or hardcore porn etc.).

I recently reread one of my books on eschatology, the study of end times, and was astounded all over again at the point where the author provided staggering statistics about the porn industry at large and the amount of porn being watched today. I will spare you the details because this is certainly not the place to share them, but let me just say men and woman and boys and girls alike are seriously caught up – quite literally speaking – in their feelings.

This is just one of, unfortunately, a long list of dangers acting based on our feelings and feelings alone can lead us to.

Freedom from Feelings

What's the danger of giving feeling too big a place in our lives? In a word, weakness.

Constantly operating in our feelings ultimately makes us weak and powerless. And to the extreme, breaks us. Because pleasure weakens self.

A significant goal in self work is to become strong and powerful. To become strong and powerful in being, body and behavior. To become a productive powerhouse. To become self-controlled and self-disciplined enough to, at any given time regardless of hurt from another person or undesirable situation and/or circumstance, direct your will and subsequent actions in such a way that you rule and overcome and continue forward progress in the direction of your short and long-term goals instead of a person, situation and/or circumstance overcoming you.

For this to happen, you must move from acting based on feeling to acting based on faith. The next section of the book, *Developing Self-Discipline*, will cover practical's and how it would look to do this.

BITE-SIZED COACHING MOMENT

1. On a scale from 1-10, before reading this chapter, <u>how aware</u> were you of acting based on feelings and not acting based on feelings?
2. On a scale from 1-10, <u>how much do you operate</u> in your feelings? (i.e., make decisions and take actions)
3. On a scale from 1-10, how motivated do you feel to move from acting based on feelings to acting based on faith more?

_____

_____

_____

_____

_____

_____

_____

Soul Work
Recap + Conclusion

This is the end of section I, *Overcoming Any Struggle*, and now, before moving ahead, it will be helpful to recap what has been covered as well as conclude – the pretty bow on top.

First, it was important for you to get crystal clear about the goal you wanted to accomplish. As a coach, I have seen firsthand over and over how not being clear is one of the biggest reasons people stay stuck and don't achieve their goals.

Second, we briefly covered the reality that struggles are a part of life. As humans we will face struggles, so we don't just wish them away we learn how to overcome them.

Third, we covered the power of visualization and we engaged you in a simple exercise to this end; with the ultimate objective being to see a clear picture of your near-future self.

Fourth and finally, we dove into a few major fundamentals for breakthrough: truth, thoughts, will and feelings – parts of your soul – hence *soul work*. And, if you did the work, you coached yourself all the way through and here you are now.

There are a several big thoughts I could share to conclude *soul work* but here are what I think are the two most vital: truth and personal responsibility.

In order to get free you must face truth. You must tell yourself the truth about your current self, situation, circumstance *and* the part you may have played. You have to get honest and take personal responsibility for who you are now and where you are now *regardless of the role others played*. This is the first step to freedom from being a victim to your struggle to being an overcomer of it. Let that sink in.

BIG COACHING MOMENT
LET'S GET CLEAR

- *This is your final coaching moment for overcoming the struggle you identified at the beginning of this section.*
- *Use GROW² to coach yourself now.*
- *This is a big moment for experiencing breakthrough. Believe it. Make it count!*

The GROW² Self-Coaching Model™

G	**Gap analysis**
	Where am I now?
	Where do I need and/or desire to be? Why?
R	**Reflection**
	What truth do I need to admit/come to terms with?
	What have I believed or accepted to be true but is not?
O	**Obstacles**
	Identify all current obstacles in your way of taking a step forward.
W	**Will**
	What decision or decisions will I make now?
	What commitment or commitments will I make now?
W	**Work**
	What do I need to do, in terms of my actions?
	What is the single most valuable and viable step I can take toward this?
	When will I do it by? Who will I be accountable to?

SECTION II:

DEVELOP SELF-DISCIPLINE

Discipline is Better

The truth is, if exercising self-discipline was easy, we would all be self-disciplined. However, admittedly while never easy, it is always the better way.

From over 22 years of studying and researching self in the context of human behavior, I personally have come to define self-discipline as *imposing rules on yourself in order to behave in a certain way*. Further, if I were asked to paint a catchy word picture to define it, it would be *mind-body behavior*.

What I mean by this is, to me, self-discipline is largely how we behave in our body. Hence, the *body behavior* part.

In my book *Self-Control*, I wrote about the difference between self-control and self-discipline because they are often used interchangeably. But there is a difference between them. In short, self-control is *on the spot* behavior whereas self-discipline is *on a regular basis* behavior.

For self-discipline, think routine. Think consistency. Think disciplined actions you take day in and day out.

With all this in mind, recall there are two major parts of Self Work: soul work and body work.

In section I of the book you engaged in soul work to overcome a struggle. Now, here in section II, you will engage in body work to develop self-discipline. For me, this is the most fascinating and fun part of Self Work because I am obsessed with *These Bodies*™ (the title of my next book) of ours.

Body work, at a high-level summary, includes your physical condition, your behavior, and your intake/consumption.

The big ideas we will be covering in this section are:

- **Self-discipline and your mind.** We can't talk about self-discipline without talking about your mind. Mental control. The mind is the control tower of all things. Any discipline, including self-discipline, starts in the mind.
- **Self-discipline and your body behavior.** We can't talk about self-discipline without talking about your body behavior. The things you choose to do over other things. Like choosing to study or write over streaming tv or scrolling social media sites. Or like choosing to have a fruit or veggie snack late at night over eating ice cream or cake.
- **Self-discipline and The Great Exchange.** We can't talk about self-discipline without talking about the Great Exchange. The required exchange of short-term pleasure for long-term treasure.
- **Self-discipline and making better choices.** We can't talk about self-discipline without talking about making better choices. There is no science to this. It truly is an art and as you began to master making better choices you will begin to experience breakthrough. You'll become unstuck.
- **Self-discipline and your purpose.** We can't talk about self-discipline without talking about your purpose, what you (your *self*) were created to become and, in turn, were created to do.

Again, this is only a list of the big ideas we will unpack, while covering a lot of other ground as well.

BIG COACHING MOMENT
LET'S GET CLEAR

1. What are your honest thoughts about self-discipline?
2. How much value do you place on becoming self-disciplined?
3. On a 1-10 scale, what is your level of self-discipline today?
4. What area of your self needs the most attention when it comes to increasing self-discipline? For this, self is the keyword. Don't consider what you do or other aspects of your life outside of self.
5. What do you want or need to get out of this section? Be SMART. State a goal or goals that is/are specific, measurable, achievable, realistic, and timely (that is, when you want to achieve your goal by).

_____

_____

_____

_____

_____

CHAPTER 8

The Mind-Body Connection

Keeping first things first, it is important for me to start helping you develop more self-discipline by making the connection between our mind and our behavior crystal clear.

I know you are well aware of the irrefutable fact that our minds control our being. That our minds control everything we see, say, and do. And not just on a philosophical level in terms of our beliefs, values, nurturing and experiences, but quite literally also on a physical, molecular cell level. Basically, how every single one of us is wired. Brain wise.

With this in mind, as I write these words, I am pondering over what thought or thoughts about the mind-body connection would have the biggest impact on you for our objective here – which, of course, is more self-discipline.

Here they are. One, possessing a particular mindset that aligns with your motivation for having more self-discipline. Two, evaluating your motivation.

(and not just "possessing" but being utterly stubborn, and strict, and rigid, and immovable in your mindset)

So, what exactly do I mean and what exactly would this look like? Allow me to use myself as an example.

When it comes down to being self-disciplined by consistently taking disciplined actions:

- My mindset is *no other option*.
- My motivation is *because of my unrelenting passion to become a better being than what I was born as in a better body than what I was born with*.
- My evaluation of this is *this means more to me than living. Which is to say, I would not want to live any other way. Which is to say, for me, living any other way would not be living.*

Do you see how much of a gamechanger this could be for you? How being of a particular mindset that aligns with your highest values work to determine what actions you, not just take, but actually *want* to take?

And there's more. When you are acting in such a way that aligns with your highest values, your actions will be disciplined ones because values tend to be good. Good for your self, your health, your wealth, and your purpose. Good for your relationships. Good for your livelihood and, ultimately, for the greater good of humanity.

How wonderful is this?

Paradigms and Body Behavior

Paradigms, (also known as mental models and mindsets), are a large part of the science that backs up the connection between our mind and actions, or mind-body behavior as I like to refer to it as.

As I shared earlier in Chapter 5, and well worth sharing again here, from Dr Richard O'Connor's book, *Rewire*, where he informs us of the recent research about how "our paradigms become part of our bodies as well. They result in changes in the brain and in other systems: nervous, endocrine, digestive, and musculoskeletal. New technology keeps improving our ability to see the brain at work, so science is very close to being able to trace the connections between thoughts and their pathways in the brain." [2]

Basically, this is the latest and greatest news in Neuroplasticity – which is the capacity of nerve cells to biologically adapt to circumstances.

Neuroplasticity is what lies beneath your capacity for learning and memory, as well as what enables your mental and behavioral flexibility.

Too, know that scientific research has firmly established that the brain is a dynamic organ and can change its architecture throughout life, responding to experiences by reorganizing connections – in short, by wiring and rewiring itself. Scientists sometimes refer to the process of neuroplasticity as "structural remodeling of the brain."

The Bottom Line (Literally)

The importance of neuroplasticity cannot be overstated. The grand significance of it – which aptly applies to our objective of increasing self-discipline – is that it makes it possible for us to change dysfunctional and self-destructive patterns of thinking and behaving (such as drinking too much, overeating, laziness, wasting time, etc.) to

---

[2] O'Connor, Richard. *Rewire: Change Your Brain to Break Bad Habits, Overcome Addictions and Conquer Self-Destructive Behavior.* Plume. 2015. Page 25

develop new mindsets, new memories, new skills and new abilities that lead to better thinking and, in turn, better behaving.

This is good news so be encouraged on your journey.

MEDIUM-SIZED COACHING MOMENT

1. What resonated with you most from this chapter?
2. On a 1-10 scale, how motivated are you to take full control of your mind-body behavior connection?
3. Identify your biggest motivation for having more self-discipline.
4. Identify the particular mindset you need to align with your motivation for having more self-discipline.
5. Evaluate your motivation.

_____

_____

_____

_____

_____

_____

CHAPTER 9

Discipline of The Mind

"Where the mind goes, the man follows" is how Christian television evangelist Joyce Meyer puts it. I have heard her say it often, but the first time I heard her say it in a sermon many years ago it really struck me, I think, because it was such a profound truth stated so succinctly. As an author, it is my favorite quote on the mind and I want to admonish you to meditate on it until you can almost feel the depth of its truth.

Creating and Maintaining Mental Checkpoints

Any form of discipline, including self-discipline, starts in the mind and if this is true – and it is – it becomes imperative that your thinking is good and right.

Always keep this in mind: good and right thinking is always your goal.

This starts with awareness and then constantly (keyword) being conscious of your thoughts and where they fall in terms of good or bad. Right or wrong. Positive or negative. Crooked or straight. However you choose to label it.

Having this awareness and intention work to create the mental checkpoints you need for maintaining the required mindset for self-disciplined actions.

Mind Mastery

Mastery of any kind is basically having complete control over something. So the notion of mind mastery would basically be having complete control over your mind.

When you study mastery deeper, you will find it involves a master-slave relationship where a "master" of some sort controls a "slave" of some sort. The master has total power over the slave. The master commands the slave what to do and the slave is obligated to do it. But it doesn't stop here. The slave is actually *trained and conditioned* to do what the master commands.

What if your mind was the master and your body was the slave? And, by our definition above, your body was trained and conditioned to do whatever its master, your mind, told it to do?

Well, news flash. This master-slave relationship already exists in you and exists in every one of us. The question is, what is your mind telling your body to do? What does your mind obligate your body to do on a regular basis? How has your mind trained and conditioned your body to behave automatically?

If you don't like your answers, consider your thinking. Has your thinking been good? Has your thinking been right? Remember, self-disciplined actions require thinking good thoughts and thinking the right thoughts.

The Power of Positive and Negative Thoughts

If you are a person that naturally thinks positive, you are blessed. If, in the face of difficult circumstances, positive thoughts come to your mind first, you are blessed.

Negative thoughts are the norm for most people. Have you ever wondered why? I have and the immediate answer that came to mind was a bit street: *because our minds are broken.*

Later I learned, science backs this up. In short, our brains have built-in biases to negativity because negativity creates a bigger charge in our brain wiring than positivity does.

Over time and with enough of them, negative thoughts can physically damage our brain by causing cognitive decline, which can lead to mental illnesses like dementia. Another way they damage our brain is by producing too much cortisol which damages our hippocampus, the part of our brain responsible for calming us down, which means we are in a constant state of *fight or flight* mode which, among other things, wears out our immune system.

So, it is vital that we are aware of this at all times and quickly recognize negative thoughts and the ill-effects they produce – some unwanted, uncontrolled, undisciplined behavior.

Fears, Phobias and Self-Doubt

At first blush it may not be very obvious, but when you think about it, all three of these are mental outflows and, therefore, can contribute to lack of self-discipline, or undisciplined behavior.

Fear, phobias and self-doubt are inherent to our human nature. Inherent to us. And because of this, it is not a question of *if* they will show up. It is a question of *when* they show up and how you will respond. So, to deny or try to suppress one of these head trips is fruitless.

Your best bet is to acknowledge but not entertain. Acknowledge the fear, phobia or self-doubt but don't take it any further than this.

And let me remind you that knowledge is power. So,

- know any fear outside of clear and present danger is mere figment and false.
- know phobias are irrational fears from incessantly giving mental energy to something sad or bad you are anticipating will happen.
- know self-doubt is lack of confidence that shows up out of a perceived insecurity within your self.

So now you know some of what stinkin' thinkin' includes. Remember, your goal is good and right thinking because both are required for consistently taking disciplined actions in order to become self-disciplined – which starts with a disciplined mind.

Your Mind and Emotions

Like everything else, your mind controls your emotions.

Or think of it like this. Your emotions are an outcome of your thoughts. Which is to say, happy thoughts produce happy feelings.

But there's an interesting twist with this. Your thoughts can also be an outcome of your emotions. Which is to say, happy feelings produce happy thoughts.

What's the deal? Here it is. Our thoughts and emotions are tied to each other.

Emotions are states of mind associated (keyword) with thoughts. They intertwine with a variety of human traits and behavioral responses such as personality, creativity, motivation, mood, temperament, and disposition to self and others.

When we think of our emotions being an outcome of our thoughts, it automatically makes us want to be more selective about our thoughts. And, while we cannot choose the thoughts that come to mind, we certainly have control over what we do with them. The thoughts we keep and the ones we discard

This discussion about thoughts and emotions is so important to self-discipline because, naturally, we are sensory beings. And, as much as I hate to admit it, we are driven and controlled by our senses.

When we are *feeling* good, life is good. Emotions are happy. When we are *feeling* bad, angry, or depressed, life is the pits. Have you been ever been here? Absolutely.

Being clearly driven by our emotions, we must master them and become emotionally intelligent. Not out of duty, but out of benefit.

I want to challenge you to become more intentional in the area of your emotions. Become more interested in them, which will beget more all-around awareness of them -- what emotion you are feeling at any given moment. What triggered it. If it is truly warranted. How you should respond to it, etc.

Too, as nerdy as it might be, take some time to find out your emotional IQ, which is simply knowing how you are wired when it comes to your emotions. This will empower you to build on your strengths and strengthen weaknesses.

As a Man Thinketh

Your mind is so powerful that it can and often does physically manifest what it thinks about.

Have you ever feared something and it ended up happening? Or been thinking about someone or something and he or she or it ended up showing up? If so, then you know what I am talking about.

You thought and thought and thought and endlessly thought about that which you feared until (keyword) it eventually manifested itself. Your thoughts created your reality. Material manifested from immaterial.

Why is this?

My personal belief is because unseen is superior to the seen. Which is to say, everything exists in the unseen before it can exist in the seen world. Before something is created or manifested it had to exist in thought form. Therefore, what we cannot see is superior to what we can see and this, in a nutshell, is why our thoughts are so powerful and the things that create our present and future reality.

In effect, we become or bring about what we think.

COACHING INTERMISSION

> Now go with me here. Take some time now to reflect and look back over the major seasons of your life up until now. Recall your dominate thought patterns and states of mind during these pivotal times in your growth and maturity. Think from then until now. What does this reveal that your current self, situation, and circumstances? Did you find it true that these are an aggregate reflection of your dominant thought patterns, that determined your actions, that ultimately determined your outcomes?

If you are honest with yourself, you will have no trouble admitting that your dominant (keyword) thoughts, particularly during difficult seasons, were self-defeating. Steeped in some fear, anxiety, hurt, habit and/or hang-up.

Know that you are not alone. Negative thinking is normal. We all struggle with negative thoughts and have suffered the consequences of them. (thank God for self work)

My issue was anxiety disorder from OCD. What started out as merely wanting to be neat, clean, orderly, and organized, over time, turned into a monstrous mess in my mind.

Mental Constructs

Mental constructs are powerful. They can do a lot of good or a lot of damage. We have to work hard to keep these constructs positive. And indeed we can do it. It first takes awareness — which is what reading this has helped with — and intention. It also takes an unrelenting commitment to not be controlled by negativity, fears, worries, anxieties, depression, anger, inappropriate thoughts, etc., but rather to have the absolute best mindset you can have.

During my recovery and healing, I made a commitment to do whatever it takes to have the best mindset that is available to me in each moment. I was fed up with stinkin thinkin and wanted a clean, clear, good, positive, wholesome, progressive, happy, strong, peaceful, calm, loving, fearless, intelligent mind. This happens with positive thoughts. Mind matter.

What I love most is, we always get to choose. And when we choose bad one moment, we can choose good the next.

It Takes Mental Discipline

So much of our daily interactions take mental discipline. Things that would not first come to mind when thinking about discipline.

For things such as:
- *Not thinking negatively but rather thinking positively*
- *Not having to be right or give your opinion*
- *Not responding to everything someone says*
- *Intentionally being quiet and not talking, just observing*
- *Not being hypersensitive and feeling sad when someone is not the first to greet you*

As well as for bigger, more substantial things such as:

- *Seeing people and situations for what they really are, not for what we perceive them to be*
- *Intentionally stretching yourself to look beyond our built-in biases*
- *Actively listening to understand someone else; their personhood and point-of-view*
- *Not allowing yourself think you're destined to marry someone you have a crush on*
- *Being slow to take offense when someone offends you*
- *To keep your peace when someone else is snapping*
- *To love anyhow when someone else is spewing hate*
- *To keep your desire for unity when someone is being extremely divisive*

This is just to name a few. I could keep listing for pages, and I am willing to bet you could easily start listing things that come to your mind as well because it is all very true!

Maintaining Mental Discipline

Given the amount of research, case studies and writing about our minds, thoughts and like things, how do we achieve and maintain a disciplined mind?

There are endless approaches. For me, it boils down to simply having right thinking. Or thinking right.

Mental models help with this and I like this approach because it is strategic – what we need to be when it comes to our thinking.

A mental model is the story we tell ourselves and the pictures we paint (i.e., every little detail) about it. They should be based on truth, but they are often based on your personal beliefs which may or may not be true.

The way in which mental models help us become mentally disciplined is, when our actions are out of alignment with our mental model, this causes a conflict that we must resolve and usually the resolution is in the form of you aligning your action or actions with the mental model in your head.

So, for example, you know what a particular self-disciplined action should be when reducing your sugar intake. You have a picture of what this action looks like and it does not involve eating a whole gallon of ice cream in one sitting.

MEDIUM-SIZED COACHING MOMENT

1. *On a 1-10 scale, how positive are your thoughts?*
2. *On a 1-10 scale, how well do you control your thoughts?*
3. *How do your emotions affect your mental discipline?*
4. *What do you need to be more mentally disciplined with?*
5. *Strategize on improving your mental discipline in the area you need to most. Determine your mental model.*

_____

_____

_____

_____

_____

CHAPTER 10

The Discipline of Self-Sacrifice

Let's just say it and accept it. Those who have made a decision and commitment to live a lifestyle of self-sacrifice are those who usually succeed at anything they set out to achieve. Their normal is vastly different from the person who doesn't live a life of self-sacrifice. What is also true is their quality of life and their income is also vastly different — better — because of it.

Did the above phrase *live a lifestyle* give you pause or did that just fly right over your head without a second thought? If it did, that's ok. Self-sacrifice is neither attractive nor sexy. But it is essential. It may not make your body feel good, but it will make your being good.

Furthermore, what good has ever happened without some sort of sacrifice? Nothing I know. And I bet you know too because you've done it. You've sacrificed self. For big things like graduating. Saving money for a house or for your child's college education. Maybe it was getting in shape to look good for vacation or a special occasion. Maybe it has been all of the above or something else.

Whatever it was, you sacrificed self and other aspects of your life for a period of time to achieve a particular outcome. Am I right?

So why not do this all the time when we know its within our capacity to? Why don't we sacrifice self as a norm?

Creating a New Normal

- ✓ If going to the gym was easier than not going to the gym, we would go
- ✓ If cooking dinner was more satisfying than not cooking dinner, we would cook
- ✓ If sitting down studying was easier than going to a party, we would study
- ✓ If eating a salad would bring more pleasure than eating gallon of ice cream, we would earth the salad

It's all about what we have conditioned and trained ourselves to and what we have associated pleasure and pain with.

So, to flip from upside-down to right-side-up, there is going to be pain involved. Pain because 1) we are righting a wrong, and 2) because of how our physical body has been conditioned to feel comfortable. Discomfort signals pain to our brain.

The key to success in turning right-side-up is you have to be willing to experience some pain for a period of time. Otherwise, you will try/fail. Try/fail. Try/fail and end up frustrated and possibly set back even further than where you started.

I am telling you this from experience. I used to be a *bonafide* snacker. Being that 75% of my pescatarian diet consisted of uncooked food, all I did was snack. After years of doing so, snacks eventually replaced full meals. Tortilla chips with guacamole as my main course and arugula and pistachios for dessert. This was my jam for 5-plus years.

When I did cook, it was a mono-meal like salmon burgers or pasta. I had long gotten out of the habit of cooking the typical 3-part meal of a meat, a side and a vegetable. For lunch, I'd have either chips and guacamole or soup and chips. With either, I'd have arugula and pistachios for dessert. And often I would have a KIND® bar for breakfast, with arugula and pistachios to make it more of a "complete" breakfast. For well over 5 years!

Radical I know. So you can imagine when the time came for me to break out and stop eating this way due to too much sodium — you think?

A constant intake of chips, guac, roasted and salted pistachios and canned soup will do that! My body went through serious withdrawal. Which translates to pain. Lots of it!

For one, not feeding my body what it was expecting and enjoyed (so I took away pleasure). Two, my habit/routine was interrupted. Three, the inconvenience of not being able to grab something and start eating immediately. Four, now having to find time and actually use it to cook a meal. All of these were major jolts of equal proportion in terms of the discomfort – pain to the brain – I felt.

But if my habits didn't change my health was at risk and "homie-don't-play-that" when it comes to her health.

By the grace of God, I was, am and will always be willing to feel some pain and discomfort for a period of time for the greater good of myself and for others.

How long your pain and discomfort will last depends on some factors like how deeply something is in you, your DNA, your general personality when it comes to the grit factor and, last but not least, your mental and emotional state in terms of your level of mastery over managing your emotions.

How to Self-Sacrifice as a Norm

It starts with a burning desire. Then decision. Then commitment to the decision. Then consistent action.

Desire is what you want. But this is flaky because our wants change with our whims depending on whatever our current mood and/or circumstance. A burning desire on the other hand is won't change. It completely consumes you until you and it meet.

Decision is making your mind up to do something. Period. You and I both know that when you make your mind up to get or do something, that is it. It's a wrap and nothing or no one can stop you.

Commitment comes down to character. It is a virtue that is not the target of mass pursuit in this day and age. But it is for some, including you otherwise you wouldn't be reading this book. Commitment is simply staying faithful. Staying devoted. All of you not parts of you. With all of your heart, mind, strength, *and* affections. You can have your head and heart in something but if your love is lacking than there is no meaning, in which case what would be the point? Just stop.

Consistent action is the practical side of these four necessities. It is the matter that puts success within reach. I would even go so far as to say it guarantees success. Whatever about failure? Yes, even with failing consistent action will guarantee success because after you fail you continue to take action until you reach success. Consistent actors have a *try until* mentality and approach. Not just try once and that's it. They *try until* they reach success.

As you operate in your new normal it, well, becomes normal. I hope you can see how huge this is. So that elevated place you see yourself operating in consistently. That place that you know you need to be in to fulfill your maximum potential and your ultimate purpose? Little by little. Step by step you will get there and it becomes your reality.

Surrendering Self: Letting Go Control

One thing about soldiers is during basic training they learn very quickly how to give up control. Quite the contrary, they learn how to submit and take orders. To be instructed. Can you imagine how difficult this must be. Because our entire lives we have been conditioned to take control. To be our own person. To make decisions. To take responsibility for ourselves, etc. Not to mention, it is in our very nature to want to have control over ourselves and lives — so much that we often take this way out of bounds and try to control others.

Soldiers no longer do what they want to do. They take orders and follow instructions. Have you ever wondered why they are made to wake up early? Because it is against the bodies natural tendency. It is a way to recondition them. When you do something enough you obviously become conditioned and trained to the point of it becoming beyond just a habit but second nature.

I am convinced that if you can conquer getting up when you naturally wake up then you are well on your way to exercising self-discipline in any area of your self and life that you want to grow in. To do this involves developing a new mental model (Remember, simply put, a mental model is just a story we tell ourselves. A picture in our mind of how something should be and/or how activity or even should go).

Practically, what this would look like is when you got up that hour or two early to maybe go to the bathroom or to take a sip of water, and surprisingly you are felling well-rested, instead of telling yourself things like *I have a long day so I need as many hours of sleep as I can get; thank God it's earlier than I set my alarm so I can* go back to sleep for... , you tell yourself *I am up and I feel good. I can take advantage of this and use the time to...*

Issues With Self

It has been rightly said that self is man's greatest hinderance. It has also been rightly said that self is the primary source of all human pain and suffering. How so? Because self is always at the root of all evildoing. When has someone ever gotten sloppy drunk or as high as a kite for someone else? Or blown up to 600 pounds from utter gluttony for someone else? Never. Because these selfish ills are done to self, by self, for self.

Now catch this. The critical thing to keep in mind about self is that, in this lifelong war you are in, self is against you. Let me repeat that. *Your self is against you.* Your body is against you. Your mind is against you. Your will is against you. Your emotions/feelings are against you. Naturally.

Think about what is currently causing you the most pain and frustration. "That thing" you need to beat. That thing that has you bound. That thing that has you stuck literally and figuratively. That thing that you are sick and tired of being sick and tired of dealing with it. That thing that if you can just break free from you will experience the breakthrough you need to be the person you see yourself as and start living the life you see yourself living. That thing that the more you will not to do again you wind up doing even more before it's all said and done.

Maybe "that thing" for you is fear like it was for me. Or maybe it's financial lack. Or worry and anxiety (me again). Addiction. Anger. Insecurity. Loneliness. Chronic pain. Chronic stress. Sickness. Disease. Obesity. Obsessions in terms of out-of-control sexual desires and/or fantasies. Depression. Lack of definitive purpose in life and the list goes on and on. And what's worst is the incessant aspect with most of these ills. These don't just show up every once in a while. No. They are always around provoking and harassing you. In fact, the harder you try to overcome, the harder the battle is with them. Can you relate?

Of utmost importance is acknowledging the truth that all these woes originate from within your self, making it clear that self is in fact your (our) biggest enemy. Really? The same self I am supposed to love so I can love others? The same self I am supposed to develop to its maximum potential?

Yes. The same self virtue and integrity flows from is the same self vice and iniquity flows from.

Now I fully realize claiming self to be our biggest hinderance is a challenging notion for most people. Why? Because it is completely counterculture. We have been raised and conditioned around self being at the center and everything else revolving around self. Further, we have been taught that self is good by the good works we do and that we must have an *if it is to be, it is up to me* mentality to make things happen.

But life has lied to you from your first breath outside the womb. Big time.

When it comes down to it, whether it was or is your own self or someone else's self (weird way of putting it I know) that caused or is causing you pain and frustration, when you peel back all the layers, you will find some aspect of self was at the center – whether your self or someone else's self.

And then there are bad habits. With these we can easily see the ills of self in operation. Smoking. Drinking. Addictions. Anger. Sexual infidelity, fornication, promiscuity, and perversions of every kind. And the list goes on and on. These mentioned are just the big ones that have no doubt affected all of our lives negatively in one way or the other.

Overcoming Self

So, the million-dollar question is, how do we overcome self? The answer is, by coming to the end of self and staying there. Which is to say, in some way, making sacrifice a part of your being.

Coming to the end of yourself is sacrificing self. Sacrificing your selfish wants for something greater. And, with this, I am not just talking about things like sacrificing yourself, your needs, your desires, dreams, your time, your money etc. so someone else you love can succeed. This type of self-sacrifice is a normal part of being in a loving relationship of any kind. Sacrifice is the greatest way we show our love for each other.

I am talking about a slightly different type of self-sacrifice. All sacrifice at its core is the same. However, there is a sacrifice when it comes to self that does not directly involve others. It only involves you. Your self. This sacrifice can look many different ways.

For example, sacrificing what you want for where you currently are. Instead of lamenting on what "should" be because you want it, and instead having an attitude of *ok this is where I am and it's not ideal and it's a hard place and inconvenient to what I want but there is something more important happening. A bigger picture than my selfish wants. There is something for me to learn while I am here.* Accepting this and if you really want to operate on a higher level of virtue, actually getting to the point where you *embrace* where you currently are.

For another example, sacrificing eating anything you want when you want. Not giving in to your insatiable appetite to eat indulgently every time you have a meal. But rather eating for nutrition 80% of the time and 20% of the time for pleasure. Remembering the good ole' 80/20 rule.

Too, sacrificing sleeping-in for serving others in some capacity. There are current studies that show people are sleeping too much. Research it a little if compelled to do so.

Finally -- and it's a big one – how about sacrificing inappropriate sexual pleasure. Stop watching pornography and watch your wife or husband with the same level of insatiable desire. Uh oh. Did I hit a nerve? This might be for you then:

- Porn is a global, estimated $97 billion industry, with about $12 billion of that coming from the U.S. (NBC News)
- "Lesbian" was the most-searched-for porn term on the world's largest free porn site in 2018. In 2019, it was "Japanese." (Pornhub Analytics and Pornhub Analytics)
- In 2019 alone, the equivalent of nearly 6,650 centuries of porn was consumed on one of the world's largest porn sites. (Pornhub Analytics)
- Eleven pornography sites are among the world's top 300 most popular Internet sites. The most popular such site, at number 18, outranks the likes of eBay, MSN, and Netflix. (SimilarWeb)
- Porn sites receive more regular traffic than Netflix, Amazon, & Twitter combined each month. (HuffPost)
- The world's largest free porn site also received over 42,000,000,000 site visits during 2019 alone. (Pornhub Analytics)
- A 2015 meta-analysis of 22 studies from seven countries found that internationally the consumption of pornography was significantly associated with increases in verbal and physical aggression, among males and females alike. (Journal of Communication 66, No. 1)
- 58 percent of men said they viewed pornography once a week or more. (Theta Wellness Center)

- 64% of young people, ages 13–24, actively seek out pornography weekly or more often.
  (Barna Group)
- More than half of all boys and a third of all girls see their first porn images before the age of 13, with "sexting" increasing in popularity.
  (Theta Wellness Center)
- In August 2006, one survey reported 50 percent of all Christian men and 20 percent of all Christian women are addicted to pornography. In this same survey, 60 percent of the women admitted to significant struggles with lust, and 40 percent admitted to being involved in sexual sin in the past year.
  (Theta Wellness Center)

We are watching a lot of porn. At home. In our bedrooms. At work. Even at school. And the results are devastating.

Jeff Kinley, author of the book *As It Was In The Days of Noah*, has this to share about the subject. "In our sex-saturated society, even preteens are being exposed to porn, contributing to curiosity, compulsion, and even addiction in their young lives.

According to the US Department of Justice, "Never before in the history of telecommunications media in the United States has so much indecent (and obscene) material been so easily accessible by so many minors in so many American homes with so few restrictions.

Pornography's impact on the degrading and devaluing of women cannot be underestimated. Today's prevailing spirit portrays women as little more than sex objects to be exploited by lust-hungry men. And apparently that's ok for some women, as long as they're considered beautiful, sexy, or desirable. A sex-obsessed culture tricks young girls and immature, weak women with low self-esteem, into thinking their personal worth comes from making men be attracted to them for their looks, body, and the highly exalted booty. What they fail to realize is that the average man thinks more about satisfying a sexual fantasy than appreciating women for who they truly are. The average man cares nothing about women as people, only as playthings. Just a means to a depraved end."

WOW.

Why did I decide to include all these stunning statistics and statements about pornography in particular? Because, watching pornography is one of the strongest appearances of what it looks like to be selfish, the opposite of sacrificial.

But all the examples I shared are self-centered and selfish in that they gratify you and you only. Notice my use of the word *gratify*. There's a difference between satisfy and gratify. When you are satisfied, you are truly (keyword) content from the better, deeper parts of you in your mind, heart, and soul. When you are gratified, it's only a temporary fix for your flesh that comes and goes fast so you have to keep repeating it. It doesn't last long because it's shallow surface level gratification.

To sacrifice something is to render actual death or the idea of death (err denial). A less dismal definition of sacrifice is to give up something valued for the sake of something else regarded as more important or worthy. Read that again.

In conclusion to this section about overcoming self, know that you will not always (keyword) overcome your self. Sometimes you will and sometimes you won't. This is just the way it is because, try as hard as we might and as much as we will, it is not within our human capacity to completely overcome ourselves. But with willingness, earnest, consistent effort, and right conditioning we can come close. So, know this. Accept this. And thank God for an infinite number of second chances.

Random thought as I am writing these very words to you: Healing really starts on the inside. It's an inside job. *#selfwork*

Moving Self Aside to Get the Job Done

Consciously sacrificing self in order to get the job done – whatever that may be.

The idea is sacrificing self for the greater good and for a greater cause in order to be better (key phrase) at getting the job done. Essential and frontline healthcare workers in the 2020 global coronavirus pandemic are a prime example.

Too, on a personal note, writing this book took my level of self-sacrifice and self-discipline to the next level. Not sleeping in and getting up to listen, read and write. To deny self- indulging in order to gain clarity about the subjects I am writing about.

Self-Sacrifice and Fruitfulness

Self-sacrifice produces massive fruit for your self, your relationships, your finances, your work and your whole life.

When you effectively recondition your mind and body from old destructive patterns of behavior that don't serve you well and operate consistently in new patterns of behavior, your world will be so full and abundant.

You will truly experience what it feels like to really live abundantly. The joy. The fulfillment. The genuine satisfaction of being productive versus fake instant gratification. Fulfilling your maximum potential and operating in your purpose using your gifts and talents.

And the more you operate like this the more opportunities you attract. It's deep and rich and it can be yours if you decide you want to live the life God intended for you and, if so, you are willing to pay the high cost of sacrificing self and doing the work. Self work.

Start Living The Big Life

Living a self-centered life is living a small life. Your world is so small when you live with self at the center and nothing else. Everything is about your own self. Your family. Your job. Your friends. Your blah blah blah (with all due respect).

In contrast when you live a sacrificial life, with others at the center, your world becomes large. Literally, the whole world become yours and you become an instrumental part of the world. A part of something so much bigger than self.

MEDIUM-SIZED COACHING MOMENT

1. On a 1-10 scale, how much do you self-sacrifice today?
2. Given the amount of ground covered in this chapter, what resonated with you most?
3. How would you explain the relation between self-discipline and self-sacrifice?
4. Why is overcoming some issue with self important to developing more self-discipline?
5. How does the idea of living an others-centered life sit with you?

_____

_____

_____

_____

_____
_____
_____
_____
_____
_____

CHAPTER 11

Body Behavior

Out of all the different aspects related to self, the body is my favorite aspect to study. I find it fascinating. So much that my next book, aptly titled *These Bodies™*, is about our bodies and is a prophetic message for the Body of Christ. But enough about this for now.

First, let me start off here by explaining what I mean by body behavior. This notion first came to me when I was in a season of wanting to experience a breakthrough that would land me on my next level self-discipline wise.

I remember, for months, having an unrelenting desire to go deeper in my disciplines. From day to day and moment to moment, almost obsessively, I would challenge my thinking on how I could take whatever discipline I was exercising at the time deeper, even just by 1%. *Deeper discipline. Deeper discipline. Deeper discipline* I would chant.

As days went on with my self-discipline deepening, it dawned on me that my "deeper disciplines" were all related to the body.

So, body behavior is the exercising of deeper discipline when it comes to your body. When it comes to our bodies.

Being/Body/Behavior

When you think about it, these three human aspects are, arguably, one in the same. How so? Because you can't separate your body and behavior from your being. And you can't separate your being and behavior from your body. And you can't separate your being and body from your behavior. They are all interchangeable.

As such, I will be using this compelling lineup of words often when normally one would expect to see them referred to separately. Let's get started.

The Art of Making Better Choices

When I was thinking about the first substantial thing I should share when it comes to body behavior – which, again, is simply exercising deeper discipline in anything that relates to your body – this is the first thing that quickly came to mind.

I want you to hear me. For me, mastering the art of making better choices has been the single-most, effective means to exercising self-discipline (and self-control for that matter). It has had the greatest impact on my capacity (keyword) for this.

What I know to be true, experientially, is that when you master making the best choice of action you should take at a given moment when you need to exercise self-discipline or self-control, you will become self-disciplined and become self-controlled. Not just exercise self-discipline or exercise self-control, but you will actually *become self-disciplined* and actually *become self-controlled.* Which is to say, you will become a self-disciplined person who exercises self-discipline as outflow from your being. And the same with self-control.

Practically, what would this look like? Let's say you are just waking up and reach for your phone to check out the time. You see the time and you also see app notifications that came in while you were asleep. Within seconds later – as a gut reaction to the notification -- you find yourself starting to open one of apps but you stop yourself and instead open your iBooks or Play Books app to read something edifying to get your day started. You demonstrated mastery by making the better choice that will ultimately work to strengthen your self-discipline.

And really important. Notice the simplicity factor. That's because this is not science. It truly is an art. And anybody can master it.

The Great Exchange

In my book, *Self-Control*, I wrote a lot more about this idea and if I had to categorize all the ideas I am sharing here, I would categorize this one as Most Vital.

What it is, in a nutshell, is when you willingly exchange short-term pleasure for long-term treasure. Exchange raw feels (as philosophers call it) for real fulfillment. Exchange quick fixes for lasting felicity.

While this may sound simple, it is much easier said than done. This exchange comes at a high cost that, tragically, not many are willing to pay. *Tragically?* I know this might seem a bit strong, but au contraire.

It's tragic because pleasure weakens and destroys. It destroys people, relationships, revolutionary ideas and innovations, dreams, potential, and, ultimately, the course of history for the worse.

Intake

First, allow me to share a sort of programming note before jumping in. This and the remaining subsections of the book will be more raw than what you've read up to this point.

I was led to write this way and feel led to share it with you this way. I believe it will have a greater impact this way versus me polishing things up just for the sake of excellent writing. For the topics at hand, I would much rather you "feel the punch" of a point over and above you thinking *what a well-written book*. You know what I mean?

Let's get started.

What I am about to share about intake has been one of the most positively impacting forces in my life in terms of affecting real and lasting change.

First it has been freedom from fear. Second it has been changing my mindset and reprogramming my brain through proven scientific methods to conquer negative thoughts and to think positively. After these two huge things is this: it literally changed me, my makeup, who I am and what I do.

Let's start off with a formal definition. Intake, in the context being used here, is the act of taking something into the body. You can think of it as bodily consumption.

One of the first things to catch with this is, intake is more than food. What you eat and drink. Intake is everything that you take in, or consume, through your five senses.

With this, you become what you consume. Literally.

When your intake is good - wholesome, pure and profitable, you will begin to experience amazing changes in your self and your life fairly quickly. Similarly, when your intake is bad, you will experience the after affects and see destructive changes in your self and life just the same.

The boundaries I have set for myself when it comes to intake is 6 out of 7 days a week, I am strict, rigid and uncompromising when it comes to my dietary consumption as well as everything else that I look at and hear. I abstain from TV, social media and other personal interests of mine. If I decide to break my abstinence during my "blackout" period, it is only for a few minutes, not hours.

Another particularly important aspect of intake is this idea of doing more of what is right. Doing more of what is right.

When you do more of the right thing there is no room for doing the wrong things. You can't do right and wrong at the same time.

The amazing thing about this is the more you do the right thing you don't want to do anything else. Why? Because of this amazing thing called conditioning. As humans, we are able to condition ourselves and our bodies.

This is huge and if you can get to the point of doing more of what is right over what you want to do, your self and your life will change. You will condition yourself to do the right thing.

I will go into greater detail about body conditioning and reconditioning coming up shortly later in this chapter.

Intake and Body Betrayal

Consider this a bit of a warning. If you don't get control of your intake – excessive consumption of food (i.e., sugar, coffee, bad carbs, processed and packaged "food"), wild sex, alcohol and drug use, hours and hours of entertainment and social media, etc. – you will not only stay at your current level but you may also subject yourself to premature death.

With this, you must get control of these things rather than them controlling you.

> *Your body is a terrible master but a wonderful servant.*

Our human bodies are, to be frank, broken and bad and therefore want what is bad for them. If our bodies were good, they would crave things that were good for it.

But they're not good, they are bad so, again, they crave things that are bad for it. And not only crave, but ferociously crave incessantly. And the harassing cravings don't stop until they are fed.

What is key for you to understand is this: that your body with its bad cravings is not your friend. In fact, it is your enemy. And, true to form to what enemies do, your body will eventually betray you — even when you give it what it wants! How scandalous is that?! This is because what it wanted and what it got was bad.

Have you ever heard of cancer? Diabetes? Heart Disease? High Blood Pressure? Blood Clots? Auto-immune diseases? AIDS/HIV? STD's? VD? Malignant tumors? This disease, that disease, etc.

You and I could go on forever naming ills that betray people's body every second of every day since the beginning of human history and until the end human history.

Like it or not. Accept it or not. These bodies of ours are not our friends. Feed it too much sugar, it responds with Type 2 diabetes. Feed it too much unsolicited sex it responds with some god-awful disease. Feed it too much fear, anxiety, worry and negative thoughts and it responds with hypertension, auto-immune disease, chronic stress and any other number of ills onset by stress.

Now the good news is you have the power to turn the tide. By mastering your body and its many ill cravings, your body can actually act like your friend. It will give you endless energy and this energy will serve as self-motivation to seize the day and make the absolute most out of it.

But just like with any training, there is a cost. A cost that most are not willing to pay. Self-denial of sensory indulgences. Too, pain to the degree of discomfort from operating outside your comfort zone and when you don't feed your body something bad it is asking for.

Just like a junkie in withdrawal goes through physical pain, so to your body will feel physical pain when you are reconditioning your cravings to crave good and not its natural bad cravings.

A helpful tip when you are feeling physical discomfort as a result of not feeding what your body is demanding you feed it, is to persevere.

So, a few things related to persevering:

1) Mindset and Self-talk. I know it's technically two things, but they go hand in hand. Know in advance that demands will show up and show up strong. So be ready and prep your mind for this advance. This gives you a real advantage because already well in advance the story you have been telling yourself will be forming your action (or lack of) come show time. Does that make sense?

2) Endurance. Outlast the craving. Knowing the craving will show up and show up strong, what you need to get good at is not giving in at the first feeling. Exercise some willpower. Now I know many of you are thinking I have zero willpower. I get it, I really do. But this is a lie. We all have willpower to some degree. Some more, some less. Some a lot more and some a lot less than others. Let me prove it. Let's say you are a smoker and you easily smoke a pack of cigarettes a day because your body addicted to and dependent upon the stimulation from the nicotine for energy (which last all of about 5 minutes, which is why you need to keep smoking them every 10, 20 or 30 minutes). If it

was true that on the very next puff you take, you will absolutely drop dead just like that, do you think you could stop cold turkey? I mean on the very next puff, as soon a hint of 1 of the 70 different toxins in cigarette smoke hit your bloodstream, you die instantly. Do you think you would have the willpower to stop cold turkey? Of course you would. This proves you have willpower.

3) Remember we prime our bodies. We condition them and train them on what to demand by what we feed them. Whatever you feed it the most it will crave it the most. Know that when we stand firm and don't give in to feeding our body bad things, know that it is not going to feel good. Don't expect it to. Know that it is going to feel funky. You will feel frustrated and irritated and dare I say get angry or downright nasty. This is true for many people. When their appetite is not fed what it is craving now or in the near future, they get really really bent out of shape. But remember, there are negative consequences to feeding your body with bad things. Body betrayal with some sickness and/or disease. Remember the negative consequences. Ask yourself right in the heat of the moment, is it really worth it? This is a great diffuser.

Finally, I want to leave you with good news. Once you get through the first several times of feeling funky as a result of not feeding your ill-appetite, it gets easier *and* you get stronger.

To encourage yourself, think of the rewards you are creating as a result of this reconditioning. Soon you will be in control (master) instead of all these bad cravings controlling you (slave). Look forward to it!

Intake and Emotions

Consider the question about how your intake effects your emotional state while I get personal and share some of my past struggles.

I know what it's like to live in a perpetual state of anxiety and never feeling relaxed. Years of living in fear and living alone devoid of connection and the intimacy that comes with being in a loving relationship is what cause the deep levels of anxiety in me. I used social media to cope and feel some level of connection to people. While I limited my time on Facebook, Instagram and YouTube, it was still too much and was information overload. Hours of looking at information, images and videos. Not realizing, all the while I was programming my mind to expect this inundation of information.

Is it any wonder I couldn't relax? When I look back on this, what is so bad is that I was aware of the fact that I was suffering with anxiety disorder and the inability to relax. I would often say out loud "I need to learn how to relax."

There were times when I would feel more out of whack than normal (depending on how stressful my day at work was the more time spent on social media), so I would be inclined to do research on Anxiety Disorder. This would always cause me to be intentional about relaxing but it didn't last for more than a few days. Now I know why. To put the psychology in layman terms, after years of behaving a certain way, my brain had been programmed such that I would behave in that way (that is, being fed a lot of information and images and, consequently, not relaxing).

Research and study for writing this book made me scarily aware of how serious (err seriously bad) this whole anxiety thing was for me. Learning the science of how our brains and bodies function was eye-opening and life changing. That my brain and nervous system was not functioning normally and that this was a huge disadvantage for me when it came to my health and well-being made me regretful and repentant.

Naturally, my goal became to undo the damage and begin reprogramming my brain and nervous system to normalcy. I remembered in my studies meditation being mentioned over and over again so I thought 20 minutes a day would be easy enough.

Wrong! My first session was anything but easy. It was a Saturday and I had cooked breakfast, studied a bit, messed with my hair and was going about doing little things here and there around my apartment. Then it hit me, *Terri your body is in a high state of anxiety right now... which is why you keep getting up moving around instead of sitting still and calmly working.*

I remember literally feeling in my body so high strung in that moment. So, I sat down to meditate. I wish I could watch a video recording to have a good laugh. The first two minutes I literally could not sit still. I was moving, fidgeting, scratching my head and kept adjusting my shoulders and hand position. (Sounds like a mental patient who has just been checked-in)

When I finally managed to keep still and not move, I decided to focus my thoughts on the ocean. Its Creator and residing creatures. Its vastness. Its greatness. Its glory. Its depth. Its beauty. Its different colors in different parts of the world. Its calm. Its power and its force and how it demands respect from any encounter with it. I wish I could say my thoughts were uninterrupted, but I can't. They started to drift on work. Then I started moving and adjusting my position again. When I was calm again I had a thought to connect deep breathing to my thoughts of the ocean. It was so difficult! My body was so uncomfortable. Why? Because it was used to being fed, thus expecting, a lot of information and images. Disturbingly, because of my conditioning, it was comfortable viewing information and images and uncomfortable sitting calm, breathing deep and creating a beautiful, serene mental picture versus seeing a digital image.

Toward the end, I lasted 18 minutes before breaking my posture and opening my eyes.

:: INTERMISSION ::

With all this talk about body behavior, intake/consumption, and conditioning, I think now is a good time for pausing to regain our perspective, which is to develop self-discipline in you. Every one of these topics relate back to this chief objective.

With this, I want to highlight the difference between being self-disciplined and exercising self-discipline. There is a difference between the two.

When you *be*, you are just being you who are. Your character. When you *exercise*, you are acting in a certain way. The way that you've trained/conditioned/primed yourself to do.

While conditioning yourself to exercise self-discipline is a great thing, the end goal for you and all of us is to become self-disciplined.

Here's why? Because when something becomes who you are, a part of your character, it stays with you and you act from who you are. Your actions are an outflow.

Military men and women start out acting and over time self-disciplined becomes who they are. My Father and every other military veteran is a testament to this.

Body Conditioning

Having your body conditioned the right way is essential for developing self-discipline. In fact, conditioning is the physical means by which you move from merely exercising self-discipline to becoming self-disciplined (exactly what we just covered during our intermission break above).

You can easily immerse – something you need self-discipline to do -- yourself in something when you've been conditioned. Trying to immerse yourself into something you are not conditioned to do is a difficult task and will often end in failure.

Your untrained body will start to feel uncomfortable when it starts to engage in some activity that is foreign to it. For example, a person who wants to start back exercising at the age of 50 after 30 years of not doing so, exercising is going to not only be uncomfortable but painful as well. The stamina or muscle strength just isn't there. So, when the cardiovascular system and muscles start working more and contracting more than used to, temporary discomfort and pain are inevitable.

Personally, even being in my 40's, if I take even a few days in a row off from exercising it is painful. And after two weeks or a month, it would be very painful and my body would be very uncomfortable.

Why is it that we can exercise consistently for so long but when we take only a short time off it is so painful? One would think since we have so much "credit" in our account this would not be the case. Right? Well the answer is surprisingly simple (at least for me). Our flesh and these bodies of ours are just plain wonky. They don't work right.

So, getting back to my main point, when you condition your body to do something, this is the point in which it will no longer feel uncomfortable. Rather, it will feel most comfortable. Athletes are a perfect example of this.

Training for the Olympics is the highest level of training an athlete can engage in. We know that what they are really doing is conditioning their bodies and conditioning their minds in what they are doing. They sacrifice every other aspect of their life and give themselves (or better said, their bodies) over completely to the process of conditioning by way of practicing (repeating the same thing) every day for years until it is time for them to perform. And, since they've been immersed, performing comes easily and they are comfortable doing whatever it is they do.

What a fine picture of conditioning and how relevant it is for self-discipline and so much more like physical fitness.

Deeper Conditioning

Most people know the power of conditioning and that to some degree or another we have all been conditioned in some shape form or fashion. Conditioned to think a certain way. Conditioned to behave a certain way. Conditioned to do certain things.

A soldier can certainly tell you all about conditioning after their basic training experience and beyond. But not just soldiers. Everyday civilians like me and you. Professional athletes. Trainers and specialty instructors, etc. We all have some experience with conditioning.

I was first introduced to the idea of Priming by Anthony Robbins, personal development guru and the guy who essentially created the coaching industry as we know it today.

Priming is a type of conditioning that is designed to condition you in a certain way (whatever your goal is) by calling you to engage your thoughts with some physical stimuli.

It promises that when you take time to adjust your thoughts and emotions through a priming routine you repeat on a regular basis, you are then able to live in your peak state.

Psychological studies for years have shown priming has a major effect on our behaviors, habits, outlooks, and emotions.

Think about a time when you were angry or frustrated – did you then overreact to a small problem? Did everything seem worse because you were still hung up on whatever made you angry? You were feeling the priming effects of your anger, which caused you to react a certain way.

Now think of a moment when you were totally in love and felt alive like never before. Did everything seem easier to deal with? Did you look at those you may not have liked in the past and felt a new sense of appreciation? That was because you were primed by the feeling of love.

The bottom line is, our thoughts, feelings and emotions can, and often are, be primed by factors we're not even aware of, which greatly impacts our performance in other aspects of our lives. Too, know that you can prime yourself negatively or you can prime yourself positively. It all depends on the quality of your thoughts and how you process them.

When practiced correctly and often, priming can help you cultivate positive emotions and drastically improve the quality of your being – including becoming self-disciplined – and the quality of your life.

Effects of Conditioning

When you stop doing bad things you've conditioned your body to, know this: it is going to be painful. Your body is going to freak out. It is going to have "fits" and experience withdrawal. Conditioning has the same affect so while you may not have been addicted in terms of a literal chemical dependency on some substance, conditioning is just as powerful. Please catch this revelation. Conditioning is key.

So, a) you must know this and b) you must decide up front if you are willing to endure temporary pain and discomfort. This is vital so let me repeat this last point: you must decide up front if you are willing to endure the temporary pain and discomfort you will experience.

Deciding beforehand puts you at a major advantage and will give you something to fight back with. Because when whatever it is rises up and wants to be fed, it is going to come strong. But with your beforehand decision to be uncomfortable and go without, it will be met with something that is actually greater. Believe it or not, you are the one in control. You just have to get to the point where your control in this area is strong which, of course, comes from exercising control over and over and over again.

So, when we condition ourselves aright in alignment with our ideal self (i.e., how we see ourself and what we see ourselves doing) we win. When we condition ourselves in the wrong ways we struggle and suffer when it comes time to get ourselves right.

Remember this: comfort equals staying where you are. Discomfort equals moving to being the person you see yourself as and doing the things you see yourself doing to, ultimately, live the life you see yourself living.

Body vs. Spirit

In conclusion of this chapter, where I have been unpacking body behavior and deeper self-discipline, I want to leave you with something different to think on.

Which is this. Realizing there will always be a war between your body and your spirit because your body and your spirit will always want polar opposite things.

The goal then is to get your body to cooperate with your spirit and the practical key to doing this is conditioning.

Know that you can condition your body to want specific things. Case and point, my addiction to eating arugula. Or, if the shoe fits, your addiction to eating whatever it is for you.

Conditioning trains our bodies, conditions them, and primes them on what to expect and, beyond what to expect, what to actually crave. Having cravings under control is what we you're aiming for.

On another note, something I love about conditioning is, it doesn't take long. Studies show it takes 21 days minimum and 66 days to really seal the deal. I am convinced this is because we are creatures of habit.

When you condition your body toward something it doesn't want anything else. But getting to this point is a process and while you are going through this process your body will "try" your spirit.

But what is so great about the conditioning process is that while you are conditioning, every time you choose what you ought to choose your spirit gets stronger and therefore it will start becoming easier and easier to say no to the bad (your body) and your spirit will actually start to win. Your spirit will start to win the battles between body and spirit.

Be encouraged!

MEDIUM-SIZED COACHING MOMENT

1. On a 1-10 scale, how happy are you with the choices you make day to day and moment to moment?
2. Going forward, how will you position yourself to make better choices in your weakest area of self-discipline?
3. On a 1-10 scale, what is your level of willingness to exchange short-term pleasure for long-term treasure?
4. What resonated most about bodily intake and conditioning, and their effects on self-discipline?
5. Going forward, how will you deepen your discipline by 1%? Map out a plan. Be strategic

_____

_____

_____

_____

_____

_____

_____

_____

CHAPTER 12

Soul Self-Discipline

Recall the aspects of your being that make up your soul. If you remember right, one of them is your emotions, also known as feelings, and they play a huge role in helping or hurting you in your striving to be more self-disciplined.

Let me make something clear from the outset. When it comes to exercising self-discipline, it is natural that you will not feel like doing what you ought to be doing. It is natural to renege on what you said you were going to do when at the time you felt like doing it.

Naturally, 99.9% of the time, you will not feel like doing anything that resembles exercising self-discipline. This is because our feelings are fallen and, as such, they naturally seek whatever feels good, is fun, easy, or entertaining. Our feelings will never long to do anything that requires denying our body of some kind of pleasure. Nor will they ever long to think through something too difficult or complex.

The casual answer to *why* is because feelings are a part of the soul, which is fallen (corrupt). So, when it comes to self-discipline, we must push pass our feelings.

First, let me say, pushing pass your feelings is, in fact, possible. You and I prove this to be true every time we don't *feel* like going to work or don't feel like doing homework or whatever obligation you have to attend to by a certain time.

Second, there is consideration of what you *have to do* versus what you *should* do. One key distinction between these two is obligation. We don't attach obligation to what we should do (i.e. exercise self-discipline in some manner). Another key distinction between these two is consequence. Not going to work or doing homework will cause immediate pain.

So, once again, the big question is how do you overcome your feelings and do what you should be doing (exercising self-discipline) when it will not cost you some immediate, painful consequence?

1. You make a decision. You decide from your mind to do it despite your feelings.
2. You do it now. You get up and do it swiftly. No overthinking. No procrastinating. Once you make the decision to do it you get to the business of doing it or moving toward it that moment.

In these two things we find an element of acting fast. Again, not overthinking and remembering results. In the moment of decision, you call to your mind what the result of pushing through your feelings or giving in to them and going the instant gratification route instead of the lasting fulfillment route.

It used to be that most times I did not feel like writing – catch this – when it was time for me to write. I wanted to write often but most times it was not when I was scheduled to write which is early in the morning between 4-6am when I feel like staying in bed. This is what my body wants. But I don't give it what it wants because I have power over it. I control it, it doesn't control me.

This is the place you want to be, and this book is teaching you how to get to this place of power and control. A place of mastery instead of enslavement.

Self-Talk Moment by Moment

What you tell yourself in the heat of the moment is critical. Your self-talk will determine your actions which will of course determine your outcome.

Sin is conceived in the mind and when it is fully formed it brings forth death. So, what is going on in the mind, your self-talk, matters most.

You must also remember this important truth: "man does not live by bread alone. But by every word that proceeds out of the mouth of God."

Bread is a symbolic of physical sustenance of our flesh. The word of God is spiritual sustenance. We cannot live on bread alone because we are body and spirit. When we live on bread alone (food and no Word), we are weak and spiritually inoperable. Likewise, when we live on the Word of God alone (Word and no food), we become weak and physically inoperable. Both equally need to be cared for and fed.

"I Don't Feel Like It"

If I had a dollar for every time I've said this or someone else said it to me I would be a richer woman.

Realize this. You will likely never *feel* like being disciplined. When you become self-disciplined, you will choose discipline but not actually feel like being disciplined. This is a space for the 1 per-center's in this life – and there aren't too many of them.

For most of us, our feelings are flaky. They shift at any given moment based on what is going on within us and around us. One minute we feel happy, the next minute we don't.

Our feelings get us into so much trouble too. Who else besides me have, for example, had a bad day at work and ended up taking it out on your spouse, significant other, child or whoever was at home when you got there?

So, our personal intention and goal needs to be learning how to master our emotions. The benefits of doing so are enormous.

Remember this: that the three big enemies you have: the world, your body, and evil forces. What I need for you to catch right here is your body, your physical make-up, is constantly working against your will to do anything it takes exercising self-discipline.

Because self-discipline is really self-denial and the body wants anything but to be denied. It wants to be gratified and to feel good.

Using EI

At the core, Emotional Intelligence (EI) is being aware of your feelings at all times and how your feelings can either negatively or positively impact your actions and reactions to what is (or is not) happening to you. And, going beyond your own feelings, it is also being consciously aware of other people's emotional state.

In her book *Improve Your Emotional Intelligence*, psychotherapist Christine Wilding provides the formal definition of EI "as a way of understanding the emotions of both ourselves and others and learning to control these emotions so that you can choose what you say and what you do, in order to engender the outcome you would like to see."

It is important for you to get the connection between your personal level of power and EI. Because your feelings influence your thoughts which dictate your actions. Which is to say if you feel happy and motivated to take action you will, however, if you are feeling particularly shitty (pardon my French) about something you won't take any constructive action. Rather you just might go into self-destruct mode.

Using EI With Others

One thing we know for sure is we have to be able to get along with each other. Outside of the big givens of loving people, accepting people, treating people fairly and justly, not judging, etc., what would be in the next category is being slow to offend and quick to forgive. And what I have personally learned after all of these huge virtues is, having the right expectations of others is vital.

First, knowing no one is perfect. People are going to mess up and people are going to offend you the same way that you are not perfect, you are going to mess up and you are going to offend people. Basically, we are all the same. We all have the same potential of good and evil in us. And God looks at you and that person you can't stand the same. He views saints and sinners the same. Truth. The Bible and evidence of living and life experience past and present proves it to be true.

Second, knowing that we all need to love and to be loved. And when this doesn't happen, doo-doo happens. The depravity runs deep. People are so thirsty for what on the outside looks like attempts for attention, but what they really are, are cries for love.

Do you for a moment think the world would be in the sad state of affairs it is in if every man, woman, boy or girl gave and received love? If everyone was in a loving, healthy, nurturing, intimate relationship of loving and being loved?

Do you for one moment think there would be as many murders, and rapes, and violent crimes if every single human being was loving and being loved? Indeed, the world would be so much "gooder" (no this is not a real word).

So, realizing the condition of humanity as a whole and that particular person that pushes all the wrong buttons on your chest. Be emotionally intelligent and have the right expectation of that person. Don't expect them to do what you would or would not do, say what you would or would not say and act like you would or would not act like.

Finally, we also cannot assume that every person we encounter is a mentally stable person. No kidding. We automatically assume everyone is playing with a full deck because most people are. However, some are not, and I am convinced this number is growing rapidly daily. Don't assume he or she is mentally stable and intelligent and can reason well, etc. Be aware. Be ready. Try not to offend and if you do forgive quickly and keep moving.

MEDIUM-SIZED COACHING MOMENT

1. On a 1-10 scale, today, how much do you operate based solely on how you feel?
2. How has your feelings hindered you from exercising self-discipline?
3. Going forward, how will you push pass your feelings when it is time to exercise self-discipline?
4. Come up with a trigger that will cause you to exercise self-discipline when you hear yourself say "I don't feel like it."
5. How will you be emotionally intelligent with others?

CHAPTER **13**

Self-Governance

At some point, a pivotal point in your journey, you will come to a crossroads with yourself and have to make an important decision on how your self and thus your life will be governed.

Who you will and will not be (your character). What you will do and will not do (your behavior). Can you think of anything else more vital than these two things about ourselves?

Naturally, we travel down the Path of Least Resistance. We naturally do what is comfortable, fun, instant, entertaining and easy instead of doing what is not fun (but the most beneficial), not instant, uncomfortable, inconvenient, harder, and even wiser.

Now don't get me wrong, I am all for convenience when it makes sense but not at the expense of long-term benefits.

The problem is when we sacrifice the long-term, truly good for the short-term, temporary feel good.

True story. I got home late from work on a Monday and was going to be having delish leftovers from Sunday dinner. I was faced with the decision of if I would take the extra time popping my snap glassware storage containers in the microwave or if I would go through transferring the food to a pot; dirtying a pot that I would have to wash; and waiting a good little while for the food to warm up before I could eat. Remember, it was late already.

What decision did I make? Without too much thinking I decided on the inconvenient route. I warmed up the food on my cooktop and later cleaned the pot and containers and that was that.

How did I make that decision? It wasn't without a struggle – as trivial as it may have been – and I had to coach myself to get me to the point of making the better choice.

What road are you going to travel "next time?" Are you going to take the easy route? Are you willing to go the hard route? Are you willing to be inconvenienced? To do what the average is not willing to do?

Once I started asking the right questions, the right response became obvious. I did not waste any more time. When I decided to *Do It Now*, in no time I was fed and finished with cleaning up the mess in no time.

BITE-SIZED COACHING MOMENT

1. What decisions do you need to make about your self?

_____

_____

_____

_____

CHAPTER 14

Food for Thought

Hunger and appetite. There is a big difference between being hungry and your appetite. Often people find themselves asking why am I hungry when I just ate? There is a strong urge to eat when they know in their mind they are not really hungry. Why is this? My belief is there is a good chance they are confusing truly being hungry with appetite cravings.

Hunger is obviously a basic function of our human body to signal when it needs food-fuel. At a scientific level, hunger happens when your stomach empties – which varies depending on several factors like food composition, your metabolism, your hormones and even your gender. But, in general, it takes 4-6 hours.

Quite differently from scientific hunger, appetite is based on cravings that, interestingly, relate to two polar things: 1) depravity and 2) over-indulgence.

When a person is deprived in some way, their appetite will crave filling the void. In the same way, when a person over-indulges, they are conditioning their body's response to the over-indulgence.

For example, eating a certain food all the time will yield an appetite, or craving, for it often and over other things.

But here's a question to consider. How can two polar opposites (depravity and over-indulgence) yield the same outcome? I personally believe this is due to the dichotomy of life. Good and evil. Light and dark. Hot and cold. Tall and short. Rich and poor, etc.

The way I see it, hunger is, by and large, a good thing and appetite is, by and large, a bad thing. Or, hungry being healthy and appetite being unhealthy. Let me explain.

When you are physically hungry it is a signal to your body that it needs fuel from food in order to keep functioning optimally. Hunger is therefore a good thing – food wise and beyond. Like being hungry to discover your life purpose and fulfill your maximum potential by using your gifts to help others.

Whereas appetite is a strong craving for something to gratify you – as opposed to something you need – and this craving is based on what you have conditioned your body to crave. And the important point to bring to bear here is, most of our appetites are bad because we've consumed, and consequently conditioned our bodies for, sinful pleasures which they did not need but merely wanted.

Let me paint a picture of what I mean.

Imagine you have two food options before you. One is a plate full of nutrition, say a wonderful salad mixed with fruits, vegetables and good carbs that will energize you in addition to satisfy you. The other is a plate of fried chicken, macaroni & cheese, green bean casserole and a side of peach cobbler for dessert. Which of these falls where?

The nutritious plate represents hunger and the non-nutritious plate represents appetite. Isn't it easy to see that your body by itself, had it not been conditioned to this or that, would be hungry for the plate of good stuff and not the plate of bad stuff? Because the body by itself was made to be fed the good stuff. It functions normally and healthily off the good stuff and breaks down bit by bit, slowly but surely when it is fed enough of the bad stuff. Poorly conditioned cravings that make up appetite in this scenario is what causes the body to want the plate of bad stuff.

If this resonates with you, start to view hunger and appetite as good and bad, with hunger being good and appetite being bad.

The next time you find yourself in a moment of decision between the two ask yourself, " is hunger driving me to choose this or is appetite driving me?"

Too, realize these two things are not going away. Hunger and appetite are a part of us. At the end of the day, you want to get to the place where you recondition your appetite to crave good things. You achieve this by consuming things that are good and healthy.

Finally, from a spiritual perspective, this is all about bringing your body into submission to your will. Bringing your body under the rule and control of your spirit. Christ taught us "the spirit is willing, but the flesh [body] is weak."

With this, know that right bodily consumption and conditioning, which determines cravings, is essential.

How Often Are You Eating?

If you are really interested in making lasting changes, now is a good time to think about how often you eat.

Ask yourself and answer honestly if true hunger driving you to eat every time you do or if it's your appetite?

After awareness of truth, reconditioning is next in terms of what you practically need to stop feeding unhealthy cravings and start feeding healthy ones.

I keep saying this and am going to keep saying it because repetition is a great learning strategy.

Our current hurts, habits, hang-ups, addictions, self-destructive behaviors, and even good aspects about human behavior boil down to conditioning. The way we have conditioned ourselves from our consumption and actions.

Earnestly think about when you eat. How many hours is it between meals? If you are awake for 16 hours a day (sleeping the other 8), eating every 4-5 hours should be sufficient for optimal energy and balance.

How long can you last after a meal before eating anything again and actually feeling fine and not flustered and ready to flip out because you "need" to eat? 2 hours, 3 hours, 4 or 5?

If you are less than 2 hours, don't be discouraged. Remember with conditioning you can get to the place where you need to be. You just having to be willing to feel uncomfortable —*really* uncomfortable — for a short period of time in order to get to where you ultimately want to be.

> *Keep this in mind: pleasure weakens while pain strengthens.*

If you are really serious about changing, you will get to the place where you will be more than willing to experience a little discomfort over short-term pleasure at the cost of staying stuck where you are.

Earn Before You Eat

If you are really struggling in this area, this strategy should help. It is simple and effective.

Exert some real energy before you eat.

The biggest issue in the Western world is, because food is so widely accessible and convenient (fast food), we are eating whenever we feel the least bit uncomfortable and/or emotional.

While researching this subject, I learned a lot of times we mistake digestion for hunger pangs. Know that there are two parts to stomach digestion: *1) mechanical digestion,* and *2) chemical digestion.* Mechanical includes rhythmic churning and grinding motions while chemical includes stomach acids and enzymes. Mechanical, as you might guess, is the one we mistake for hunger pangs.

Make it your goal to eat only when your body (keyword) is hungry. Not when your mind and mood – which are components of appetite – are being harassed by some nagging craving.

People perish and are destroyed because of lack of knowledge. So now that you have the knowledge, it is your personal responsibility to make sure you apply it in order that you will not only survive but thrive.

Artificial Stimulants

If you are among the masses who consume artificial stimulants, you may disagree, but you do not need these to live.

Let me prove it to you. Do they literally wake you up and get you out of bed? No.

I know many of you believe you need to consume some artificial stimulant first thing in the morning, however this is only because of the story you tell yourself.

You've told and continue to tell yourself things like *I need this to make it. It gives me the boost I need. This is good for me. What would I do without this. I've tried but I can't function without this. Nothing else gets me going like this, etc.*

I get it.

But what you've really done and continue to do is convince your mind and condition your body to the point that you are now chemically dependent and crave what you've convinced and conditioned yourself to crave. Whatever your stimulant of choice.

So first you have to tell yourself the truth. The truth is you do not need artificial stimulants to get you going. You may want them but you don't need them. The life/vitality in you is what physically awakes you and gets you going. The stimulant does not. It is your mindset, will, emotions, speak and physical/energy exertion that control this.

And just like your mind and will can be bent toward artificial stimulants, they can also be bent toward right conditioning and natural energy and zeal to get you through your day, activities, events, etc.

Don't ever underestimate the power of enthusiasm. It is more powerful than any artificial stimulant you can consume.

MEDIUM-SIZED COACHING MOMENT

1. What truth or truths do you need to admit?
2. On a 1-10 scale, how would you rate your self-discipline when it comes to eating?
3. What eating habits have you been wanting to change but have not yet reached success?
4. Have you gained new insights that would help you reach success in this area? If so, what are they?
5. What will you commit to going forward?

CHAPTER 15

Making Up When You Mess You

By this point in the book, if you started reading from the beginning, you should be experiencing significant progress in overcoming a struggle and developing more self-discipline. However, know this: you are a human being made of flesh not stone. Because of this, it is not a matter of *if* you mess up but *when* you mess up.

In fact, there is a good chance you have already found this to be true. But, if not, it would be wise for you to know about this possibility in advance so when it happens you won't be too hard on yourself.

This being said, when you mess up, what do you do? How do you handle yourself then? Two great questions.

Must Do's

There are a few things I have found that are must-do's:
1. Remind yourself of how far you've come and all the progress you've made.

2. Remind yourself that you are an imperfect human being living in an imperfect world and with this comes difficulty. Bad days are inevitable and to be expected and accepted. Life is tough and we are all trying to make it through. Declare: *I am not alone in my struggles.*
3. Acknowledge your error and make a commitment with yourself to be better and do better. Strive for excellence in this error. Take the time to actually picture yourself operating in excellent order the next time around. Paint the picture. Make it as vivid as possible. This is a powerful exercise because by doing this you are creating a new mental model that your actions will inevitably conform to.
4. Ask yourself what you can do right now to move on and upward from the mistake you just made. *Right now* is the key here. While it is certainly true that tomorrow is a new day and often used as a starting over point, I personally believe in something I think is even better — the power of now. Doing something now that is counter to your misstep will lift you up now. It will shift your energy from negative to positive now. Not later but now, which is what you need. It will shift your mindset by not giving your mind a chance to dwell on what just went wrong. It will start the process of putting this in the past in your mind. Powerful indeed. Deciding to wipe the slate clean and do something to counter your misstep now will move you from a place of defeat to a place of power and self-control. When you do something now you will feel so much better afterward. It will be like your own personal, sweet redemption. You will feel a healthy sense of pride, accomplishment, and fulfillment because , even though you may have messed up, you made something good out of it in the end.

Don't Do's

Similar to the list of must do's we just covered, of course, there is also an opposite list of don't-do's so you will not hinder your progress as you work to reach your goals.

Here they are:
1. Don't fret. Do not kick yourself while you're down
2. Don't stop. Do not stop taking the right actions because you slipped up
3. Don't dwell. Do not dwell on your mess up. Doo-doo happens to the best of us
4. Don't be discouraged. Do not take the bait of the bin of negative emotions that come so naturally. Resist
5. Don't magnify. Do not make your mistake out to be something more than what it was.

BITE-SIZED COACHING MOMENT

1. What will you commit to do and not do going forward?

_____

_____

_____

_____

Body Work Recap + Conclusion

This is the conclusion to Section II, *Developing Self-Discipline*. The biggest idea to remember and keep in mind from this section is that developing self-discipline falls under Body Work – one of the two parts of *Self Work* (soul work and body work).

Second to this, I want you to remember and keep in mind the main objective in developing self-discipline, which is for you to actually become self-disciplined as a result of exercising self-discipline.

In other words, self-disciplined is who you are as opposed to something you do or exercise – although exercising it is certainly your starting point and means to becoming it.

I also want you forge ahead on your journey knowing:

- Self-discipline (body) is an act of your will (soul). The unseen is superior to the seen. I need you to catch this revelation.
- Focus on your end goal, not what it takes to get there.
- You must determine the person you want to become then get about the business of becoming that person with unrelenting passion.
- You absolutely must set the standard for your being/body/behavior and commit to living uncompromisingly to it that standard– no matter who or what when it comes to yourself and others.
- The Great Exchange -- have you settled the matter? It's a must.

Finally, I would love to tell you to believe in yourself, because it sounds good, and to a slight degree you do need to believe that you do have the capacity (keyword) to become self-disciplined. But this is minor in the grand scheme of things. The bigger necessity to lay ahold of is knowing self-discipline is about making a decision, then making a commitment from the decision you made.

BIG COACHING MOMENT
LET'S GET CLEAR

- *This is your final coaching moment for developing self-discipline with your ultimate goal being to become self-disciplined.*
- *Use GROW² to coach yourself now.*
- *This is a big moment to grow&go higher. Make it count!*

The GROW² Self-Coaching Model™

G	**Gap analysis**
	Where am I now?
	Where do I need and/or desire to be? Why?
R	**Reflection**
	What truth do I need to admit/come to terms with?
	What have I believed or accepted to be true but is not?
O	**Obstacles**
	Identify all current obstacles in your way of taking a step forward.
W	**Will**
	What decision or decisions will I make now?
	What commitment or commitments will I make now?
W	**Work**
	What do I need to do, in terms of my actions?
	What is the single most valuable and viable step I can take toward this?
	When will I do it by? Who will I be accountable to?

SECTION III:

FULFILLING YOUR MAXIMUM POTENTIAL

Your Highest and Best Self

This section is last for good reason. Because in order to fulfill your maximum potential you, your *self*, must be free and must have self-discipline.

It is impossible for you to fulfill your maximum potential when you are wrestling with some struggle with self. Just like it is impossible to fulfill your maximum potential without self-discipline and some aspect of self-sacrifice.

My purpose is to lead others to transformation by helping them become their highest and best self in order to fulfill their maximum potential. Key phrase, *in order to.*

The reason we strive to become our highest and best self, or another way I like to put it is, to become something better than what we were born is, is so we can fulfill our maximum potential.

Potential is on the same level as purpose. Reaching your maximum potential means you are operating in your purpose.

Can I be honest? I never once expected to be as passionate as I am about maximum potential. I mean, it's a great aspect of personal development but "self" has always been my thing. But, as the story of my life unfolded, I became passionate about it as a result of myself having years of wasted potential and thus feeling like a failure behind me. All those years I knew I was not operating in my maximum potential. Haunting and frustrating describes it but, what's worse is, I eventually came to view it as a gross dishonor to my Creator and gross dishonor to my purpose – the very reason I was created and consist.

Allow me to help you not have a story like mine.

BIG COACHING MOMENT
LET'S GET CLEAR

1. Are you fulfilling your maximum potential? If not, what is standing in your way?
2. What are your honest thoughts about potential? Are you apathetic about it?
3. Given your age, race, gender, education and other factors, do you feel like it's too late for you? Is this God's view?
4. What is your biggest frustration?
5. Are you allowing your past failures to hold you back, because you feel guilty, worthless, or some other negative view of yourself?

_____

_____

_____

_____

_____

CHAPTER 16

Identifying Your Thing

Let me ask you, what is your thing? The single most important thing you should do every day to either operate in your purpose or move you a step closer to operating in your purpose?

The expression, "being all in," came to my mind when thinking about this idea of your thing because this is exactly how you have to be. All in.

When it comes to your thing, being *all in* is getting to the point where you realize very few things are more important than doing your thing.

Outside of taking care of family, working and primary responsibilities, nothing else is more important.

Being all in also causes you to realize something that takes the majority of people nearly their entire life: we don't have as much time as we like to think we have. We convince ourselves we have more time than we actually have.

When you come to these realizations you will have a sense of urgency and with a sense of urgency driving you, it will be easier to resist the temptation to "not feel like it today" or to choose doing something else fun, easy or entertaining over exercising self-discipline to do your thing.

Discovering Your Purpose

Potential is tied to purpose. When you begin to operate in your maximum potential, you will automatically begin operating in your purpose.

So many people overthink their purpose and make it more complicated that it needs to be. I get it. I've been there.

But now I know better and have since learned one of the main reasons why people (unintentionally) complicate it.

There is a sneaky element of fear that is coming into play. Specifically, FOMO – fear of missing out. People want a guarantee that if they label one thing as their purpose, they are not missing out on the possibility of something else being their purpose and thus missing it.

But the truth is, identifying your purpose is not complicated. If you don't already know yours, here are some statement prompts to help you identify it:

- Purpose is tied to duty, or responsibility.
- We all have personal responsibility to become something better than what we were born as.
- Your purpose, in a nutshell, is to become your highest and best self then share yourself with others.
- Your purpose is directly tied to how you were made.
    - Who you were made to *become*.
    - What you were made to *do*.
- How are others better when they cross your path?

Your Golden Goal

This is ultimately about identifying your reason for wanting to overcome any struggle, develop self-discipline and fulfill your maximum potential.

There has to be a reason attached. Your *why*. Or what I call your golden goal. It is golden because you will have other goals, but this is the one that lies at the root of all others.

Think of your golden goal as your ultimate (keyword) purpose for living. For example, my ultimate purpose for living is to teach truth. So, every goal I set should involve me teaching truth in some shape, form, or fashion.

Teaching truth is my golden goal. It is my *why* and my motivation for doing self work to overcome any struggle, develop self-discipline and fulfill my maximum potential. It is what drives my actions. It is the primary reason I do what I do when I do it. With a sense of urgency.

MEDIUM-SIZED COACHING MOMENT

1. Clearly state your purpose.
2. Clearly state your thing and explain your why.
3. Clearly state your golden goal.

_____

_____

_____

_____

CHAPTER 17

How to Start Thriving

Does this word invoke a feel-good sensation in you? It does for me. I love this word. I love seeing it. I love saying it. I love its dictionary definition and especially love the meaning attached to it in the context of maximum potential.

To thrive is to proper or flourish. It's an action word. Some synonyms that paint lovely word pictures for it are: *do well; develop well; grow vigorously; go well; grow rich; make strides; bloom and blossom.*

I don't know anyone who would not welcome and embrace these into their being and behavior.

My intention here is to share a diverse mix of "knowledge nuggets" that will help you thrive, and thus fulfill your maximum potential.

The Shift

This is what you want to happen and where you want to be.

The place where you no longer even desire to do the things you used to do and you can't wait to go about doing your thing.

The point mentally, and therefore in your actions, where doing your thing is more important than sleeping, eating, being idle, indulging and/or entertaining yourself streaming movies, endlessly scrolling through social media feeds, etc.

Have you gotten to this point? If so, you've had a major breakthrough to fulfilling your maximum potential. If not, imagine and keep imagining yourself being here. Keep doing the work and you will arrive in due time.

Being in Flow

The power of Flow is astounding. When thinking about it and defining/describing it to others, I like to use the phrase, *the force of Flow*, because it moves and propels you to action.

According to *Simple English Wikipedia*[3], Flow is a term used in psychology to mean the mental state of a person completely immersed in an activity. It is an altered state of consciousness.

The person is fully focused, performing actively and successfully. The situation is widely recognised by phrases like in the zone,[1] in the bubble, on the ball, in the moment, wired in, in the groove. The performer almost loses touch with their surroundings: phrases like "lost to the world" reflect this mental absorption.

The term flow was given to this experience by a psychologist, Mihaly Csikszentmihalyi. He said it was completely focused motivation. The hallmark of flow is a feeling of spontaneous joy, even rapture, while performing a task.[2] Flow is also described as a deep focus on nothing but the activity – not even oneself or one's emotions.

---

[3] https://simple.wikipedia.org/wiki/Flow_(psychology)

Ebb and Flow

Still when you've identified your purpose and are operating in it, and have gotten to the point where very little matters before it, because you are *all in* and have made a commitment to doing that which you are called to do and the very reason why you consist daily, there will be times when you are in full flow and there will be times when you are ebbing (err struggling).

Attribute it to the dichotomy of life (good evil, hot cold, rich poor, etc.) and expect it. Just stay consistent in terms of taking action –exercising self-discipline, sticking to your routine, etc. – and before you know it you will begin to flow again. Just because you might be ebbing stay immersed. Keep doing what you should be doing, and I can almost 100% guarantee you will be flowing again in no time.

Focus

The ability to focus is one of the most valuable skills you can develop in the digital world of distraction we live in today.

It is impossible for you to be *all in* without being able to focus — to stay single-minded — for an extended (keyword) period of time.

Given how much time I used to spend on social media, I have had to do some serious work in order to develop laser focus. Through my study of it, I've learned that the physical makeup, or matter, of our brain is adversely affected by a constant bombardment of images, words and sounds that the endless feeds social media sites and apps give us. It's referred to as Sensory Overwhelm. To our brains, it is literally information overload.

Words by themselves — books, articles, educational material, no matter how it is packaged — have always been and will always be good. It's the images that have such a profound impact on the physical makeup of our brains. Because of the shapes and colors. We are visual learners. Pictures are the most powerful in our learning. It is how we are wired; literally how our brains are wired.

So, think about this for a minute. If we learn visually and are constantly seeing images that are of no substantial educational value, what is that doing to us? To our mental processing and subsequent behavior?

Here's something to think about. If the images are not educating us, what exactly are they doing?

The answer is, changing the way we think, process and — catch this — changing our focus!

Remember conditioning. In the same way we condition our body, we are conditioning our brain to receive a constant feed of sights and sounds so when it comes time to focus, we literally can't.

Do you see the severity of this problem, err pandemic?

Now that you know, resolve to stop feeding the madness - literally because if it is not educational then there truly is no point and no profit to your brain consuming it. It's actually harmful.

The last point I will make about focus is, it also extremely important when it comes to being still. When it comes to prayer and meditation that creates and strengthens calmness in moments you need it most. If you're not able to focus, the quality of your prayer and meditation won't be there. Which of course defeats the whole point.

Identifying Your Motivation

Identifying your personal motivators is important in order to keep moving forward. If you don't have the right motivation, when (not if) adversity strikes, you will be stopped instead of being unstoppable.

People that are propelled by the right motivation are unstoppable. When they run into adversity, they remember their motivation for doing what they are doing, and they push forward.

Research shows the best way to identify your motivation is to align them with your top values. And, in our context of self work, be sure to categorize your values *Self* and *Life*. We commonly, to a fault, leave self out and only focus on values associated with things (albeit major) in life outside of self.

Being Self-Motivated

We know that motivation is what drives you. Scientifically, there are different kinds of motivation and many psychological theories about it.

There is intrinsic and extrinsic motivations, which draw the line between motivation that originates within your own self and motivation that originates from an external source.

Self-motivation is superior.

To fulfill your maximum potential, you must arrive at the point where you don't need any person or any outside influence to motivate you to take action. In this way you are under the control of that thing — which could be good or bad.

Remember, personal power is your ability (keyword) to take the right action. Really catch this.

Yes, I will concede, something is better than nothing (i.e., being extrinsically motivated), but strive for best, and best in this case is you getting to the point where your motivation is pure and from within because of your own passions, decisions and commitments to becoming your highest and best self. Then to bottle it up and give it away to others so they can do the same, and so on. Make sense?

Tapping into the Power of Routine

Mostly all of us have a routine of some kind already. Whether it's getting yourself and/or your children ready for work and off to school. Whether you do you preparation at night or follow a certain rhythm and flow in the mornings.

There are many studies that show every person who has reached an extraordinary level of success has a routine. Michael Jordan, the most prolific basketball player of all time, attributed his success on the court to his routine.

Routines do three things for us and in us: (1) strengthen our self-discipline; (2) produce habit in us; and (3) refine our technique through the power of its repetition.

This is the stuff that success is made of.

On another note, know that when you do get a routine, you will need to protect and guard it closely. Because when (not if) you get off your routine for even one day, you are going to feel the negative impact of doing so. How so? Because it takes 3x positive to overturn a single negative.

This is why we can go to the gym and train our mind, body, and soul for 365 days straight but when we go astray for, say, a week we experience significant setback.

Or like the idea of not being able to "catch health" but we can catch a disease. There is just something wonky about our bodies. They are broken and don't work right. We struggle tremendously in them even when we do everything right. Can you relate? Have you figured this out?

This is why it is so vitally important for us to train and condition and possess the kind of gritty approach of "go hard or go home" when it comes to training and conditioning our bodies. The more we do the better off we are and the easier we will bounce back when we're knocked off our routine.

Every Moment Matters

This is absolutely true. Every single moment of our lives matters greatly. Or better said, what we choose to do with every single moment of our lives matters greatly. The first thing I want you to catch here is the keyword choose.

Years ago, I read a scripture that indicated we would be judged for every idle word spoken. This was back in the day when I was a babe in Christ and I was newly on fire for God.

When I read this scripture, it put some holy fear in me. *Wow*, I exclaimed. *Every word*? Every word. *I better watch my mouth.*

Between back then and recent years, my awe of this scripture – as much as I hate to admit it – had waxed cold. Until now. Having experienced more of life, made more mistakes, matured and gained more wisdom, I realize it is absolutely true.

First and foremost, because all scripture is true (this is my personal belief), and second because it has *proved* itself to be true.

Every significant (keyword) word I have spoken in this life has had a consequence — immediate or delayed. Real or imagined. Good or bad. I believe every significant word you have spoken has had a serious consequence.

Quite literally and figuratively, words create our worlds.

So how do words relate to every moment mattering? Because in the same way every significant word has a consequence, every significant action does. And every significant action you choose to take is one that is profitable or not. Every significant action you choose to take is adding to or subtracting from you and the quality of your being and life.

Setting the Atmosphere

Sticky notes, vision boards, banners, books...

Whatever reminds you of your thing, surround yourself with it. Put yourself right in the middle of these things. You will draw an amazing amount of energy and inspiration from them.

This is because we are such sensory beings. Anything that enlivens our senses works to an advantage for us. This is true whether good or evil input (can you say revelation?).

So, when it comes to being in all and setting your atmosphere, it's really about bombarding your senses with input related to your thing.

It would be ideal if you could set the environment in your home but if this is not possible then find a place. Go wherever you need to. Get creative.

The Art of Finishing

In naming this section, I decided to use the word *art* instead of the word *habit*. Reason being, art evokes positive emotion.
The word habit, because of bad habits, carries potential to evoke negative emotion.

Art is defined as *a skill at doing a specified thing, typically one acquired through practice*. Habit is defined as *a settled or regular tendency or practice, especially one that is hard to give up*.

The commonality between the two is *practice*.

Both art and habit require practice – doing something over and over again with the goal of becoming proficient. Think Picasso. Beethoven. Michael Jordan. Michael Jackson. Michael Phelps and an endless sea of artists, thinkers, and high performing athletes.

A few top, common reasons why people don't finish what they start:

1. **Lack of Urgency.** You know as well as I do that when something urgent comes up you jump on it and take care of it immediately. You go through whatever lengths to take care

of the situation that could cost you money or cause you to waste time, experience some painful consequence and inconvenience.

2. **Lack of Self-Discipline.** A simple definition of self-discipline that has always stuck with me is from Brian Tracy. He describes self-discipline as *the ability to do what you are supposed to do, when you are supposed to do it even when you don't feel like it*. Most people live under the control of their feelings. This is detrimental because our feelings usually work against us and not for us. We feel like eating and indulging in things that are not good for us. We feel like sitting on the couch or surfing the Internet and Social Media feed for hours. We feel like

3. **Lack of Personal Power.** Personal power is your ability to take action. This certainly applies to not finishing what you start because you don't take consistent (keyword) action. The will for you to take action is there. So is the desire. But will and desire are not enough. Adding conviction is not even enough. You need personal power – the force that gets you moving and empowers you to keep moving in spite of everything else.

4. **Stuckness.** Stuck because of some fear. Or some worry/anxiety. Or some insecurity (lack of confidence). Or some pain we are in. Or some addiction that consumes your mind and thus your actions.

Sir. Madam. Young man. Young lady. It is time to get real with yourself and identify which of these shoes fit in order to resolve and remove every roadblock in the way of you finishing what you've started now and in the future.

MEDIUM-SIZED COACHING MOMENT

1. Have you made The Shift yet?
2. What is your Flow? When are you in Flow?
3. On a 1-10 scale, rate your current capacity to stay focused on what you are doing for several hours straight?
4. Would you consider yourself self-motivated?
5. Do you have a daily routine or do you go through your days reacting to however the day goes?
6. Do any of the common reasons why people don't finish what they start apply to you? If so, come up with your game plan to resolve the issue(s).

_____

_____

_____

_____

_____

_____

_____

CHAPTER 18

Handling Resistance

When you start to thrive, you will also start to experience resistance. Seen and unseen. Obvious resistance and not-so-obvious resistance. Overt resistance and covert resistance.

Did you happen to notice how many times I repeated the word resistance? I deliberately did this because I want you – your self and psyche – to get used to the idea of resistance like you are used to the idea of forward progress in life. Setting and achieving goals. Organizing and planning your next short- or long-term move to level up. How you can be better today than you were yesterday. Etc.

In other words, I want you to always keep it in mind. Not obsessively, of course. But, again, in the same way you think about the things I just mentioned.

Why? Because you (we) will always, always experience resistance. It's very nature and essence is incessant.

Do I have your full attention now? I sure do hope so.

Forms of Resistance

The moment you make a decision to do *your thing* no matter what – to make it a top priority outside of your personal responsibilities – you are going to experience resistance. Internal and external resistance, seen and unseen.

Let's start with unseen because it's the superior realm.

Internal unseen resistance can show up in the form of criticism, insecurity, fear, doubt, or any other variety of negative emotion. You will ask yourself questions like *what's the point? What am I doing? Who do I think I am?* And make statements like *I can't do this. This stinks. This isn't good enough. I'm not good enough. I will never be good enough. This is too big.*

External unseen resistance can show up in the form of strong physical urges to do something else. Anything else besides doing your thing. You may also experience some physical pain or minor discomfort. Know now, with this particular resistance, you are just going to have to push through it when within your strength to do so. Ignore it and enter into your state of flow. You will be glad you did because, my experience has been, it passes after its been resisted. All of a sudden, you're good. What's more encouraging is, the more you do it, the easier it is to do it because you are strengthening your muscles in this area every time.

External seen resistance can show up in the form of distractions (things and people), sudden urgent situations and circumstances that call for your attention (i.e., your car broke down, your refrigerator went out, someone broke in your house, etc.).

The ability to still take action when you are experiencing resistance is personal power at its finest and to say this will serve you well at present and in the future (if you keep operating in this way) is an understatement.

Why Resistance Shows Up

I wish I could tell you factually why this is. I can't.

But my personal belief is, it has a lot to do with the dichotomy of life. Since I've mentioned this several times already, you might be thinking, *this again?* Yes. The dichotomy of life is pervasive and prevalent in just about everything.

When attempting to comprehend it, think good and evil. Hot and cold. Happy and sad. Tall and short. Rich and poor. Pride and humility and the list goes on.

From a theological perspective, the Bible teaches evil is always present when you determine to do good, and this is actually a law that is at work at all times (see Romans 7:21-23). This is the way it is because of the knowledge of good and evil.

So, knowing that, when you determine you are going to do something good, it is natural, aligned and to be expected that something or a slew of things will start happening to work against you.

The good news is, overcoming resistance and staying on course is a skill that can be developed. Also good is the fact that when things start coming against you, you get to choose how you will react - whether you will allow yourself to be stopped or if you will ignore them and carry on with the business of doing what you determined to do.

What I know for sure is, you can overcome resistance if you are willing, and if you possess a little grit, and if you are committed to achieving the goals you've set and, honestly, if you are just downright frustrated and/or disgusted with your current condition and at the point where you will let nothing stand in your way.

Because you've been here and done that. You've wasted too much time and know that now is the time to keep taking action until you reach your goal. *Until* you reach it.

True story. When I determined to sit down and write this chapter after a long day of demanding IT work at my corporate job, my routine productivity activities, coaching, and later cooking, cleaning and getting organized, I was feeling low on energy and actually sleepy. Still, I declared aloud that I was committed to achieving my goal (which I had set earlier in the morning while mapping out my day) of writing and completing another chapter. I declared *I have the energy I need to reach my goal*. After the right self-talk I was ready.

Then what happens? I walk into my bathroom and find a bug hanging out over one of the mirrors and, of course, it absolutely had to be squished immediately. In chasing the bug, I knocked one of the covers off the vanity light and couldn't get it back on (spent 10 minutes on this). As if this wasn't enough, I started smelling something fishy. Literally, this foul odor came out of no where and it threw me way off trying to figure out where it was coming from (which had never happened). So, I walked out of the bathroom determined to sit and write. I'm in position ready to write and my iPad is running slow. Then I notice my iPhone case was coming apart on one side. *Really?* is all I could think to myself.

So finally, frustrated (there's that word again), I hurriedly set the phone face down and made sure it was on silent so I would not be disturbed. I began to write and thoughts and words began to flow.

When you show up, miracles and amazing results happen.

Evil Resistance

I debated on whether I should go here or not in this personal coaching guide, but I have to. This is something that we all face on a daily basis. Therefore, you need to know about it and be equipped to handle it.

My highest hope is for you to develop a keen and shrewd aware of evil resistance so you can id it and be strategic in overcome this ugly, evil reality that too often hinders or altogether stops good from happening.

Evil resistance exists because evil exists. It's this simple.

And another particularly important thing to know is it is evil resistance is always working, or always in operation because Good is always at work and the working of evil is to oppose Good.

Both Good and evil work incessantly. With this, Good is at work in a given person, people, situation/circumstance or evil is at work in these.

When Good is at work, evil resistance shows up. So, the question becomes, how do you (we) overcome it?

1. **Acknowledge that evil exists.** Where there is good there is a good chance evil will show up
2. **Ignore it.** The biggest thing that evil wants to do is to control you. To possess you. And how it goes about that is to get into your mind. Because again where the mind goes the man follows. If evil can get into your mind it knows it can then have control over you.

To not allow this you have the option of ignoring evil. Remember, giving someone the silent treatment. Completely ignoring them acting as if they don't even exist. Well this is a very effective strategy in dealing with evil forces that show up that are not of your own doing, thoughts and out of your control. Just ignore them. Evil always has an end in mind and that end is the destruction of everyone it can suck in. Don't fall for it. Don't respond to evil. Ignore evil. Now in order to ignore evil — and overcome it which I will speak on next — you yourself have to not be evil. Because like responds to like. Everything produces after its own kind.

3. **Overcome evil with good.** In order for this to happen you have to be good. You have to be in alignment or on the side of good. Like responds to like so if evil shows up and you are evil then you will just respond to the evil because that it who you are. On the other hand, if you are good and evil shows up, your response to evil is good because you are good. And — get this — good trumps evil. Good is superior to evil. Why? Because God is good. Further, God created good and He also created evil.

Practically, this looks like your character. Good being demonstrated in your character — what you do in private and public. The way you think. Your beliefs and values.

4. **Change your view.** If at all possible, don't look at this as something that is happening to you. Look at it as something that is happening around you. When you look at it as something that is happening to you, you make yourself a participant in it. Whereas if you look at it as something that is just happening around you, that completely changes your feelings about it.

5. **View it as an opportunity to become better.** Something else that also comes into play is the fact that this is an opportunity, a challenge, for you to look at a situation differently. To not look at something that is an adversity but rather to view it as an advantage. Radical I know but stay with me. If you want to turn a negative situation on its head than don't play into it. Go with it. When you resist

something, you fight against it and the resistance gets stronger and stronger. Whereas when you go with something and don't resist then eventually there is no resistance. The Law of Resistance needs two opposing forces.

So, view this as an opportunity for you to grow and gain mastery over yourself. Your soul, which is the seat of your emotions, but it also includes your mind and will which is a great thing. Gaining mastery over your thoughts is also good.

6. **Surrendering yourself.** Meaning removing yourself from the equation. Taking yourself out of it. This is closely aligned with not viewing yourself as a participant. Just surrendering. Disconnecting from your own pride, ego, self-awareness and resigning yourself to the fact that life is bigger than you and what is happening close to your world is what it is and knowing that you don't have to have anything to do with it. It is what it is and that's it. Just surrendering to life. In life there is good and evil. Just surrendering to life for what it is. Having the right expectation that evil will show up. Everything will not always be good and when it is going good for a certain period of time appreciate that but when evil comes accept that and just make sure you are do your part to not participate with the evil. Again, overcome the evil by being good yourself and doing good yourself – to the extent that you can and not worrying about or being concerned about the actions of other people.

In conclusion, consider Christ. He was able to forgive because there was no offense in Him. Because He was not only full of forgiveness, He was forgiveness. Now we of course are not Christ. We are mortal men and women and it is a challenge for us to not get offended and when we do to be quick to forgive.

But there is something else that is important to point out here. And that is, Christ was sent for evil doers. Outside of Him being forgiveness and no offense found in Him, He was sent for the very ones that were doing evil to Him and who would ultimately kill Him. He was sent to them (and everyone else in the world).

My point in highlighting this is perhaps, by all evidence, you are sent to the person that is the source of evil toward you.

Or if not sent, then to some lesser degree but still you have a part to play in that persons healing and/or deliverance.

Or to even a lesser degree, perhaps you just have a very small part to play in this person's journey to becoming their best self. And in order for you to play your part and not disrupt and/or sabotage the bigger thing that God has in mind for both you and that person, you need to respond with good, thereby overcoming evil.

Extreme Self-Discipline and Resistance

Sometimes to overcome resistance what is needed – and the only thing that will help – is exercising extreme self-discipline.

There will be times when you have to push yourself to exercise extreme discipline in order to get everything done you set out to do. Extreme discipline in the sense of not being lenient on yourself but rather being rigid when it comes to sticking to your routine and plan.

Of course, there will be times when things happen outside your control, at which times you have to be flexible to adjust plans and go with the flow. However, there will also be times (the majority) when things are in your control and you have to exercise enough discipline to stick to your laid out plans no matter what.

This reminds me of being a Communication major in college when I had to take several journalism courses. In my TV journalism class, as a news reporter we had to put together packages. Those packages had to be a certain length and if a package was over or under the length requirement by even a second it could not be used.

Now you may think, well sure because this is a very technical thing. And this would be right. Nevertheless, it makes my point that to operate at a higher level to achieve your goals, when things are solely in your control, at times you will need to be strict like this in order to overcome resistance. This is the very essence of self-discipline.

So, what does this look like? One example would be if you lay out your day's schedule the night before planning to do one task at a certain time for a length of time, then another, and another and so on. Once your time for the first task is up, you hard stop and move on to the next regardless of if you finish or not.

If you have been making some progress toward where you want to be but feel a little frustrated because you are not getting there at the pace you want or think you should be, exercising extreme discipline may be the missing link.

Remember, you are always up against some form of internal or external resistance, seen or unseen.

MEDIUM-SIZED COACHING MOMENT

1. What about resistance resonated most with you?
2. How has something you learned in this chapter helped to explain past or present contention?

3. Are you now able to look back in hindsight and identify resistance that was at work in a particular situation/circumstance?
4. Choose your strategy for overcoming evil resistance.
5. Does the use of extreme self-discipline compel you to look forward to when you need to exercise it?

_____

_____

_____

_____

_____

_____

_____

_____

_____

_____

CHAPTER 19

Having More Energy

After, by necessity, covering such a joy kill topic like *Handling Resistance*, and in the spirit of ending on a high note, let's have some fun and get into *Energy!* What you need to know, how to have more of it, and how to use it to help you start fulfilling your maximum potential.

Doesn't just the thought of it energize you? That's the power and amazement of it, which is exactly why we need to tap into and leverage it in our bodies and lives.

As with anything, we must be intentional about our energy if we are to have enough energy to carry out our purpose.

Have you ever given earnest thought to energy being an integral part of operating in your purpose? Well it is. Because you have to have the energy to carry it out.

This may not sound very profound, but it actually is.

The Importance of Energy

For me, there cannot be enough emphasis placed on energy. Few things are more important when it comes to personal empowerment, and this is what you could call a "basic need" when it comes to taking action and operating on your highest level while doing so.

Yesterday I was meditating on energy. How critical it is when it comes to fulfilling your maximum potential, and how this is the thing that holds many people back from operating at the level they should be operating on were it not for lack of energy.

You have everything you need in terms of the knowledge, the will, resources, courage and boldness but when it comes time to work on your hustle, you're tired. Winded. You want to sit down or lay down and relax. You need to recharge because your energy tank is empty.

One of the key thoughts from my meditation is God is our ultimate source of energy. What an awesome thing, I thought.

When we remember He is our source of energy we should get very excited because He is of endless supply. And not only is His energy endless, it is all-powerful. Unlike anything artificial we can pump ourselves with, the energy He provides is pure and powerful.

We just have to a) recognize our true Source; b) receive Him as our source of; and c) tap into it.

One thing that is true is, the older your body gets the more it takes for you to be energized versus someone with a younger body. Older bodies have been through more and the truth is parts start breaking down. Nevertheless, when we think right and eat right and have good over all intake, our actions will be right what they need to be. All of these things working together will create a field of energy that will empower you.

Let me share a story that paints a powerful picture on the importance of energy.

I used to work with a guy – really nice guy -- who smoked a pack of cigarettes a day. To say he was addicted to nicotine would, yes, be an understatement but it also wouldn't be the full story. He was addicted and dependent on it. It was so bad that he needed to smoke every 20 minutes in order to get through his workday. If he didn't smoke, he wouldn't make it. Due to the effects of nicotine and poisonous toxins, his body no longer produced energy on its own from food nutrients and other natural factors such as rest and rejuvenation.

What was fascinating to me was how bright and intelligent he was. When I tell you smart, I mean smart. This guy was a wake and walking brain when it came to what he did, which was data cubing and modeling. Not only this, he was a sales and marketing genius. Not only this, he was an accountant. Not only this, he had keen business acumen as well as common sense.

We would often talk about side hustles. Our passions. What we were called to do. I'd share mine and he would share his bright ideas – and they were truly bright.

The sad part was (can you guess?) he never followed through on any of his ideas because he simply did not possess the energy. His lack of energy ended up being a major hindrance to him fulfilling his purpose and maximum potential.

Energy and Mindset

In contrast to my coworker's energy plight, which was more physical, mindset also comes into play with energy. A lot of having the energy you need is mindset.

How many times have you not been your best when you woke up but had an important meeting or event that you had to rise to the occasion and be your best? You had to give yourself a pep talk right to get yourself in the right mindset. Have you ever been there? Probably a better question is, how many times you've been here. I know this is certainly true for me.

Energy and Action

Just take action. Just do something. Do what you can right now. Don't delay. Be wise and proceed with caution. Don't be hasty and seek counsel. Pray before you make moves. But don't not do anything.

When you take action you create movement. With enough consistent actions, momentum is created.

As I am sure you know, momentum is a force. So even with taking little actions consistently, the force of momentum will help you keep moving.

Please catch this. It is very powerful. And what I love is all you have to do is a little something. Just do something.

That little thing will get bigger and bigger and bigger until your goal is met.

If you have an idea for an invention, turn the thought into a reality. Begin to manifest your idea by making the smallest move. Then another. Then another, then another. The small actions will build up and momentum — the force — will be with you.

Energy and Enthusiasm

I bet you have at some point in your life been around someone whose enthusiasm was absolutely contagious.

Enthusiasm is "next level" positive emotion, and it creates an enormous amount of energy. So much so that not only is the person with great enthusiasm energized but also everyone else around them. Really think about that. What makes that happen?

The word enthusiasm comes from two Greek words: *en* meaning *within* and *theos* meaning God. So, the word enthusiasm literally means *God within*.

Remember above I shared God is our ultimate source of energy? I am convinced this is how one person's energy (the God within them) is contagious to the other people around them. Because the life of God, *zoé*, another Greek word, is within us all.

Enthusiasm has for a long time been one of my go-to emotions. When I would feel sad or down in spirit, I would make myself laugh out loud or go to a mirror and see myself smile with the biggest smile my mouth could make.

When I would feel nervous or insecure or afraid, I would call on enthusiasm to curb my nerves. It worked every time in disarming them.

When I was tired and as a result not operating at my best, I would be enthusiastic. I didn't need a shot, a drug, some external artificial something to energize me. Enthusiasm did and still does it for me every time.

Always remember enthusiasm energizes. Also remember, the evil resistance always at work against you wants nothing more than to rob you of your enthusiasm – and your love, peace, happiness, joy and anything else good. Fight back and attack consistently with enthusiasm and evil won't stand a chance in hell to get an upper hand on you.

12 Great Ways to Increase Your Energy

The way to increase your energy at any given time is to exert more energy. To move around and/or exercise more.

Here are a few of my favorite ways to increase my energy when it comes to body movement – which is different from working out with the intention of getting a great burn.

1. Take a dancer's move dance class. Talk about high energy? Yes

2. Take a cycling class
3. Engage in a deep breathing exercise for 5 minutes. Because of the short period of time, really make it a great session
4. Put on one of your favorite tracks and dance to the music. My absolute favorite.
5. Pretend like you are a boxer and beat the air while bouncing around.
6. Sit up straight and sit up away from your chair while you work.
7. Shake periodically for 60 seconds. Keep shaking nonstop.
8. Do some Jumping Jacks.
9. Do some leg extensions. Several rounds and kick as high as you can. This energy-gaining exercise is real. It will energize you to 100.
10. Take up an active sport like playing tennis.
11. Take the stairs.
12. Walk, jog, or jump rope in place.

Remember, your overall intake is important, and everything factors in when it comes to your energy level. Movement is just one factor.

MEDIUM-SIZED COACHING MOMENT

1. *On a 1-10 scale, rate your energy level today?*
2. *Do you need to adjust your mindset in any way when thinking about the different aspects of energy covered?*
3. *Pick your go-to emotion on occasions when you need to increase your energy?*
4. *What action(s) will you commit to doing consistently to create momentum to achieve one of your goals?*
5. *Pick a way to increase your energy. Will you commit to doing this for 5 minutes a day?*

_____

_____

_____

_____

_____

_____

_____

_____

_____

Maximum Potential Recap + Conclusion

This is the end of section III, *Fulfilling Your Maximum Potential*, and before going any further I would like to congratulate you on finishing the main sections of the book.

In my estimation, and I hope you agree, we covered some pretty good ground here. Starting out with identifying your thing – the thing that keeps you from sleeping in and going to sleep at night. Then getting into thriving in your thing. Next, we moved into handling resistance that is always working against you, be it through people, situations/circumstances and even organizations and systems of government. Then, finally, topping things off with an all-important discussion about energy – the amazing, vital force that causes us to create and move and accomplish anything we set our minds on, big or small.

After all this, I cannot think of a better way to end this sort of lecture on fulfilling your maximum potential than by sharing practical, actionable steps for you to do just that.

    A. **Set yourself up for success.** Plan in advance. Set your goals that morning or the night before

    B. **Become obsessed with achieving your goal.** The more you set goals the more you will get into it and get to the point where you obsess over it. It becomes fun and challenging which is always good and healthy. You start to focus on the outcome and not necessarily the process (which is usually a lot of self-sacrifice, self-denial, self-discipline and discomfort). You will stop focusing on the process and focus on the your desired results. And when you actually start seeing results in your being and life, you will never want to quit and think why it took me so long to get to this point.

C. **Commit to your goal.** If you are committed to your goal, there is virtually nothing that will stand between you and achieving your goal. It's like when your heart gets set on something, or when you make up your mind to do something. Few things will stop you from doing what is in your heart to do.

D. **Show up.** Not just when you have resistance but because you have resistance. In other words, change you mindset and the way you look at the resistance. Determine that the resistance is a good thing because just by it being present you know you are doing something right. Shift your mindset and not only accept the resistance but embrace it . Use it as motivation to start and finish your goal all the more.

E. **Put in the work to achieve your goal.** Remember, personal power is your ability to, not only take action, but to take the right action.

F. **Express gratitude for enthusiasm.** *Theos*, or the God within you. This is divine enablement to help you make things happen.

Let's keep at self work and reach success together.

Cheers!

Terri Andres

BIG COACHING MOMENT
LET'S GET CLEAR

- This is your final coaching moment in this personal coaching guide that was created to help you in overcome any struggle, develop self-discipline, and fulfill your maximum potential.
- Use GROW² to coach yourself now.

The GROW² Self-Coaching Model™

G	**Gap analysis**
	Where am I now?
	Where do I need and/or desire to be? Why?
R	**Reflection**
	What truth do I need to admit/come to terms with?
	What have I believed or accepted to be true but is not?
O	**Obstacles**
	Identify all current obstacles in your way of taking a step forward.
W	**Will**
	What decision or decisions will I make now?
	What commitment or commitments will I make now?
W	**Work**
	What do I need to do, in terms of my actions?
	What is the single most valuable and viable step I can take toward this?
	When will I do it by? Who will I be accountable to?

ABOUT THE AUTHOR

TERRI ANDRES is a woman of great passion, purpose and influence who has given her whole self and life to service. At the age of 23, she was radically saved and transformed into a brand new person through a supernatural encounter with God. Today, Terri is a formally trained minister in the Christian faith, a gifted communicator, leader, visionary, entrepreneur, and philanthropist. When she is not working, she is resting and enjoying life with her loved ones.

ABOUT THE AUTHOR

BRI ALDORES is a woman of great passion and enthusiasm in everything she loves. For years she and her husband at the age of 21, she lost her son. She cried and cried, she cried herself to sleep. Through happenstance, hope, faith and cloud, faith, family, friendship, trust, belief, hope in life, Christian top. She is a compassionate leader, a smart entrepreneur, and an influencer, who shares her strength. She is loving, and he loves life with her loved ones.

Visit **harvester-publishing.com** for more premium self-help products and also follow us on Facebook @*harvesterpub* and Instagram @*harvesterpublishing*.

Self-Control: Power to Experience Breakthrough, Transformation and New Life

Living with self-control means living with power. Self-control is what makes the difference between knowing what you should do and actually having the ability (the power) to do it. This paperback book is 297 pages of knowledge that is guaranteed to change your life!

The Self-Control Grocery Shopping List

This is an indispensable tool for optimal health and well-being when it comes to your dietary intake and weekly grocery shopping. Never again will you have to give a lot of time and thought into what you should try and buy next to make you feel and look your best every day.

Self-Control Habits: 30 Habits That Take You Higher

In this powerful eBook you will learn strategies that are easy to incorporate into your everyday routine that will break bad habits such as laziness and procrastination and energize you in the areas you need it most.

www.ingramcontent.com/pod-product-compliance
Lightning Source LLC
Chambersburg PA
CBHW012207090526
44583CB00022BA/2935